Mourad Mazouz

THE *momo* COOKBOOK

A Gastronomic Journey through North Africa

Recipes by Abdallah El Rgachi, Richard Meyniel
and Eva Edery

Travel narrative by Janine di Giovanni with

additional text by Eva Edery

Food photography by Jean Cazals

Travel photographs by Mark Luscombe-Whyte

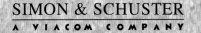
SIMON & SCHUSTER
A VIACOM COMPANY

First published in Great Britain by Simon & Schuster UK Ltd, 2000
A Viacom Company

Paperback edition, 2004

1 3 5 7 9 10 8 6 4 2

Simon & Schuster UK Ltd
Africa House
64-78 Kingsway
London WC2B 6AH

Managing editor: Susanna Clarke
Text design: Jane Humphrey
Cover design: Ocean Blue
Typesetting: Stylize Digital Artwork
Stone backgrounds kindly provided by Kirkstone, Fired Earth and Paris Ceramics;
photographed by Steve Baxter; and produced in Adobe Photoshop® by John Errwood
Printed and bound in Singapore

A CIP catalogue record for this book is available from the British Library

ISBN 0 68486 010 4 hardback
ISBN 0 74326 372 3 paperback

contents

OPENING A DOOR TO NORTH AFRICA

My heart, my sensibilities, my emotions, my memories, my passion and, above all, my love for North Africa are all that I could draw upon to write these pages. It is with this palette that I sketch a portrait of North Africa: my own.

It unveils, little by little, the best that our countries have to offer in the art of entertaining and the art of living – with all the paradoxes of tradition and modernity.

I have a profound desire to share with you what North Africa inspires in me, and this I present in all humility. If you already know North Africa, I hope that this book will give you the pleasure of rediscovering its heritage and its riches. If you are discovering it for the first time, I hope that, through these pages, you will overcome the feeling of distance by having within your reach a guide to the diversity of the region and a taste of its customs and its cuisine.

My single ambition, throughout this book, is to make it a tribute to the five senses of the reader. Morocco, Algeria and Tunisia all share a common talent to inspire the senses of the traveller. It is with a light touch that I wish to fly you over a typical landscape of flavours, sounds, colours, smells, images, anecdotes, customs, traditions and rituals.

What is undeniable is the beauty with which nature has endowed these countries, the wealth of their cuisine and the boundless hospitality of their people. In these countries, the cuisine resembles the landscapes: it is warm, colourful, aromatic, subtle and mysterious. Contrary to the ideas of the uninitiated, the subtle harmonies of herbs, spices and smells combine delicately and without aggression to caress the palate.

Though certainly different from European cuisine, the North African table does not include any rare or obscure ingredients. It relies upon inexpensive products: lots of vegetables, fruits, cereals, meats and poultry which are easily obtainable but which, with the artful use of spices, herbs and fragrant waters, can be transformed into marvels. Different combinations of the same basic ingredients can be used to produce infinitely varied results.

North African food is simple to cook and does not preclude the use of one's imagination. It is quite acceptable to replace quinces with apples or pears, or pigeon with chicken. The recipes that are reproduced in this book are genuine, although I have deliberately left out all those, however delicious, that may upset the western palate. I have not included *rate farcie* (stuffed lamb spleen) – a great delicacy of Jewish Moroccan cuisine; chicken's feet with chick-peas, garlic and dried red peppers; lambs' brains with saffron, lemon and coriander; the famous sheep's head cooked in red sauce; or *osbane*, a thick tripe sausage found in Algeria and Tunisia. I have also had to leave out recipes requiring vegetables which are hard to find in western

My single ambition, throughout this book, is to make it a tribute to the five senses of the reader.

Clockwise from top left: tile; date seller outside Marrakech; blue door in Chechaouen; pomegranates in Tunisia

countries. So, regrettably, I have not been able to include *guernina*, a vegetable of the cardoon family; white truffles; *slaouia* squash; and the delicious little violet artichoke with needles, so common in Morocco.

There are two great communities – the Arabs and the Jews – which have lived as brothers in the countries of the Maghreb; two communities for whom holidays mean times of sharing, marked by the exchange of gifts, pastries and congratulations; two communities which cultivate traditions of mutual respect and tolerance, hospitality and friendship; two communities which celebrate the tradition of blessed and shared bread, family traditions, superstitions and identical ceremonies. These twin traditions are underpinned by twin cuisines in which only religious laws make any difference.

Great festivities greet the birth of the firstborn son in both communities: these are circumcision, *mila* for the Jews and *khtana* for the Muslims. Though these events take place at different ages, they are celebrated with the same ritual and accompanied by a great festive meal.

Food for one is enough for two, and food for two is enough for three.
Arabic proverb

Weddings encompass many ceremonies and may take up to a week: the day of the *henna*; the day of the trousseau; the day of the *hammam* or ritual bath; the day of presents; the wedding day itself; and the *achat el hout*, a fish dinner given by the newly-weds to their family and friends a few days after the wedding.

At funerals professional mourners, the *nouwahat*, are employed by the bereaved family.

Pilgrimages are celebrated with ritually sacrificed lambs: *moussem* for the Muslims and *hilloula* for the Jews.

North African cuisine is a generous cuisine. It is generous like the mother and prodigal like the son. The nature of the people of the Maghreb is demonstrated in the love, generosity and hospitality offered to friends, parents and guests.

There, cooking is an act of love, a feminine act celebrated with joy, song, good humour, and the famous *youyous* – a cry of celebration – when cooking for the holidays.

It is a cuisine that is a gift; it is abundant and nourishing like a mother. Despite the abundance placed on the table, one always hears at the end of a meal: 'But you have eaten nothing.'

It is a region where even the poorest eats to satisfy his hunger. The Koran and the Bible alike invite us to share and to give. Walking one day in the *medina* of Marrakech, I learned that every day a certain restaurant served a free bowl of smoking-hot *harira* to the poorest people, free of charge – a charity for which a rich benefactor paid. But generosity is not confined to the rich. I remember my appetite being stimulated by the smell of freshly baked bread carried from the oven by a small boy. My request for a small taste was answered by being given a whole loaf as well as an invitation to his parents' house to share a glass of mint tea and home-made pastries.

I remember when I was invited to the home of a wealthy businessman in Marrakech. Whilst we waited for the meal, he showed me around his beautiful garden full of the rarest exotic flowers and cacti. By the swimming pool, I admired a wonderful fireplace in *zellige*, the traditional Moroccan mosaic. I innocently asked him if it was for barbecues. We sat down to lunch and, after a multitude of delicious little salads and hors d'oeuvres, there arrived an assortment of fried fish from Safi on the coast, caught that very morning. I thought that this was the climax of the meal when a huge assortment of grilled kebabs, *kefta* and lamb arrived. At this point my host confessed that this course was not on the original menu but in my honour, he had asked his cook to add it at the last minute so that we could sample the produce of the barbecue

In our land, there are as many couscous as villages, as many tagines as vegetable gardens, as many desserts as orchards and as many recipes, jealously guarded, as families.

that I had admired! Only one hour had elapsed between my innocent enquiry and the presentation of this feast. I still do not know to this day how this miracle was achieved!

These are just a few examples of the limitless generosity of the people of the Maghreb, rich and poor alike.

The cuisine of North Africa is voluptuous, a sensual feast. It presents its abundance in a carnival of colours, perfumes and flavours. In our land, there are as many couscous as villages, as many *tagines* as vegetable gardens, as many desserts as orchards and as many recipes, jealously guarded, as families.

Our cuisine has power: it has the ability to stimulate as well as to satisfy your appetite. It has the ability to warm as well as to refresh. It can enchant, captivate and, even more amazingly, it has the precious ability to heal. The cuisine reflects the people of North Africa. It is piquant and sweet at the same time. Sugar and salt, spice and honey ride together happily in tandem. It also reflects the influences of the different peoples who have at one time or another inhabited the area: Berber, Arab, Jewish, Ottoman, Italian, Spanish and French.

Smells and colours guide the steps of the visitor: the smell of freshly baked bread rising from the oven, the aroma of charcoal-grilled lamb emanating from a little corner restaurant and the fragrance of huge bunches of fresh mint hanging in the marketplace. According to oral tradition, the way to learn to cook is to observe; the only instrument of measurement is the eye.

Cooking in North Africa is an art beyond the simple process of preparing food. It is the art of taking time to live, the art of taking time to do what needs to be done, and, equally important, the art of presentation. I am thinking, for example, of *znanat* (an Arabic word meaning 'gardens'), a festive hors d'oeuvre that reaches the summit of refinement in the art of presentation. *Znanat* is made up of beetroot (deep purple), parsley (green), carrot (orange), egg yolk (yellow), egg white (white). All the ingredients are prepared separately and then formed into the shapes of flowers or stars, rather as a gardener will plant his floral display. Because the use of the human form is forbidden in the Muslim world, the artists of the Maghreb have become skilled in reproducing their calligraphy and arabesque in infinite variety.

I invite you now to step through the door that I open for you, to enter the world of the Maghreb, its customs, anecdotes and recipes. But all the while, I wonder if what I really wanted to share with you is just a bit of nostalgia for my happy childhood in Kabylie.

Mourad Mazouz

Mourad Mazouz

The Land, the Food,

In Morocco there is a proverb, 'Here, you eat with your eyes'.

Walking early one morning in the ancient *souk* of Fez, I think of this. The air, even at this hour, is thick with the smell of cumin and roasting meats, but it is the visual assault that is the most staggering. Everywhere I look, there is colour: fat purple aubergines so dark they look bruised; piles of stark white garlic; bundles of bright carrots just pulled from the earth. Next to the carrots is an ancient, stooped man selling cloudy jars of preserved lemons; behind him a woman with hennaed hands and feet and a tattooed face is selling bags of dried lavender, sacks of deep crimson and purple rose petals and tube after glass tube of *khol* in deep blue, green and lavender. The palette – purple, green, red, orange – is so strong, so intense that the stalls resemble a Gaugin still life.

the People

North Africa is a region of contrasts. One passes from a desert of sand to a desert of stones; from a lush oasis to a moonscape; from a sun-kissed seashore to snowy mountains; from a medieval village to a twenty-first-century megalopolis where a camel waits patiently for his master in front of a cybercafe.

Like the South of France, there is a certain quality to the light here, which combines with the tactile sensuality of the land. The Maghreb is compelling and yet disturbing in its beauty: the smells, the tastes, the textures and the colours are more potent than an opiate.

There is a frightening intensity to desert landscapes, as Kit and Port, the protagonists of Paul Bowles' classic novel, *The Sheltering Sky*, tragically discovered. When the Italian director, Bernardo Bertolucci, decided to film this novel, he shot the opening sequence in Tangier and the long, desert passages in the Algerian and Moroccan Sahara because he wanted to capture the haunting ambience of the novel, the theme of outsiders living in a disturbingly beautiful place.

Many artists, writers and painters have chosen to live, work and create in the Maghreb. Albert Camus, when writing *L'Etranger*, chose the themes of exile and of a man's alienation within an overwhelming culture. Another writer and adventurer, the young Russian-Swiss Isabelle Eberhardt, travelled the Maghreb extensively beginning in 1897 and made some shrewd observations as she roamed. 'The sumptuous green and silver curtain of olive trees falls back on all these fleeting visions,' she wrote lyrically from Oujda in March 1904, 'on this dream of a few hours, made up of both intoxication and nightmare.' Eberhardt was only 19 when she escaped her provincial Geneva upbringing and came to North Africa. She fell in

> He who is unable to prevail against his mother-in-law takes vengeance on his wife.
> Arabic proverb

love with the region and spent the next eight years wandering through the desert towns with the nomadic people of the Saharan region of Morocco and Algeria. She was only 27 when she died in a flash flood in the Sahara.

It is impossible not to feel the allure of these places. At sunset on a cool autumn night, standing on the roof of an old house in the *medina* of Marrakech, I watched the sky descend into darkness. Extraordinary colours: first the crimson of the horizon, then the subtle slashes of pink, blue, purple and finally the richness and

Scenes from Marrakech central market

blackness of the night. The edge of the city seemed to fade away and from my perch I could hear the distant calls of the vendors at Djemaa El Fna selling hard-boiled eggs with cumin, fried fish, dates, figs, lemon juice, roasted meat on the spit and glasses of mint tea. I could smell the strange mix of overcrowded sewers and the jasmine blossoms – always strongest at night. I could see the edges of the minaret and waited for the *adhan*, the call to prayer which comes five times a day and that is central to the Islamic faith.

THE NORTH AFRICAN PEOPLES AND THEIR LANGUAGES

The people, like the landscapes, are diverse in the extreme, from the *Sahraoui* (the people from the Sahara region) who are very dark skinned to the people from Kabylie who have fine features and pale-coloured hair, skin and eyes; from the *Touareg* who are extremely tall to the Arabs who are small and very brown.

The region retains the linguistic influences of its many occupiers. Besides Arabic, Berber and French, Spanish is widely spoken in Algeria and in the north of Morocco, and Italian in Tunisia. The Jews of Tangier call the Jews of the rest of Morocco *los forasteros* (the strangers) and their Judaeo-Arabic dialect, *Khaketiya*, is peppered with Spanish expressions, each one spicier than the next, which sit happily in the same sentence with Arabic and Spanish words.

SUPERSTITIONS AND MAGIC

Superstitions, exorcisms and legends have always been part of the lives of North African people and even today old customs and beliefs remain embedded in the psyche. Practices to ward off the evil eye are too numerous to list as are the ways of attracting good fortune. The *khamsa* (literally 'five'), generally symbolised by the hand of Fatima is a ubiquitous symbol in the Maghreb. It appears in silver or gold, depending on whether it is worn on the body or is guarding the baby's cot, the house or the shop. Sometimes it is accompanied by banknotes for extra good luck. The Tunisians add an eye, against the evil eye, and a fish to counter bad luck.

Early morning camel market

Ceremonies are held where sandalwood (*houd*) or other mixtures (the *bkhor*) are burned in order to frighten away evil spirits. Herb shops and spice merchants (*aatarine*) do a busy trade in all sorts of herbs, woods, stones, roots and dried bodies of animals, which are believed to have magical powers. Certain women (*gazzanat*) have made this their trade and will deliver advice, concoctions, amulets and magic rituals to encourage fertility, good luck, luck in love or the acquisition of riches.

WATER AND BATHING

The people of North Africa have a peculiar and highly important relationship with water. They perform their ritual ablutions several times a day. Every town and village has beautiful *zellige* (mosaic) fountains to provide drinking water and a place to wash one's hands before and after meals.

The sensual ritual of the *hammam* (the public bath) is an integral part of life in the Maghreb. The *hammam* provides a place where people can meet, talk, refresh and beautify themselves. You can get a henna tattoo or take a mud bath with *ghassoul* to revitalise hair and body; you can have endless massages with perfumed oils or be exfoliated by the *tiabates* wielding a special abrasive glove. And when you are finished you lie, enveloped in a robe, on a divan in the relaxing room of the *hammam*, drinking a glass of mint tea and eating honeyed pastries.

> The Emir's dog died. Everybody sent his condolences. The Emir died. No one paid any attention.
>
> Arabic proverb

Woman drinking from a fountain in a mosque, Fez

THE FOOD OF NORTH AFRICA

The Maghreb is a rich place. The land is fertile and the growing capacity is vast. The food shows the influences of all the different peoples who, at one time or another, have settled here: African, Islamic, Arab, Berber, Ottoman, French, Italian and Spanish.

Each of the three countries that make up the Maghreb – Algeria, Morocco and Tunisia – has its own particular style and flavour of cooking and the three tables are different, though they share lots of common recipes. Tunisia, like Libya, has been heavily influenced by Italian cuisine. Algeria was part of the Ottoman Empire until the French arrived in 1830, and so has strong Turkish and French traditions. There is a noticeable Andalusian influence in Moroccan food, particularly in the parts of the country closest to Spain.

A North African Meal None of these influences has changed the basic elements of Maghrebi cuisine. A *tagine* is designed to cook all the ingredients – meat or fish, vegetables and sauce – at the same time, unlike a typical European meal in which these elements are cooked separately. A typical North African meal is not presented as a starter, a main course and a pudding, but rather as a main dish with numerous side dishes and desserts.

An Abundant Table Abundance and tradition are the common themes that bind together the food of Morocco, Algeria and Tunisia. Early European visitors were taken aback by the amount of food set on the table. 'Everyone knows the Eastern nations prefer fatness to leanness,' wrote Dr Arthur Leared, who published his observations on Morocco in 1876, 'In Morocco, the taste for obesity principally affects the fair sex. Ladies must be fat, for such is the will and the pleasure of their Lords and Masters.'

This taste for voluptuous women which prevails in the Arab world generally, is born of a desire to demonstrate good health, an abundant table and by extension give an impression of opulence. The ideal woman in the Maghreb is curvy, white-skinned, modest and, to please her mother-in-law, shy. Skinny women are referred to as 'a candle dressed in a skirt' (*hska labsa saya*), the ultimate sign of disapproval.

The Hills are full of the Bounty of God

Even in the villages and small towns, people can eat well with what they forage. The hills of the jbala (mountain people) are plentiful.

Al-Haj Mohammed is a pedlar who lives in a village in northern Morocco where his ancestors have lived for generations. He says, 'The hills are full of the bounty of God. Life is hard in the hills, but the hills are full. We grow wheat, barley and broad beans in the valley fields after the start of the winter rains in October. We harvest them in early summer, after the death of the land (*mut del-ard*) in May. In the winter we sit around the *mijmar* (an earthenware brazier) fanning the charcoal embers and drinking hot mint tea. We listen to the rain pounding on the roof and pray that it will not wash away the wheat. We grow tomatoes, potatoes, green peppers and mint in the village gardens in the hills. We have figs, plums, apples and pears from our village orchards. We have buttermilk, butter and cheese from our goats and our cows. We have the meat of our goats, the eggs of our chickens and fish from the sea.'

In the country and in the mountains where the *kasbah* (hamlets made of *pise* – a red mud mixed with straw) are numerous, the roles are clearly divided. It is not rare to see the women, including the eldest, cultivating the fields and carrying enormous bundles of firewood on their backs or children carrying water from the nearest fountain or spring in an assortment of the most extraordinary metal or plastic containers.

Everyday family meals are often very simple. In the poorest the poorest families very little meat is eaten. Meals always include fresh bread accompanied by whatever may be to hand. There might be olives, dates, olive oil, *merkha* (a yellow sauce made with oil and spices in which one dips the bread) or a *harira* made of wheat or barley (which will be called *frik* in Algeria or *belboula* in Morocco). *Lben* or *raib* are often prepared at home from goat's or cow's milk.

Street Food

At any hour you can find something good to eat in the city streets or on the corners, on the road or in the *souks*. A huge variety of foods are sold from small carts or improvised tables. There are *brochettes*, bowls of snails, *harira*, little fried fish, sheep's heads, orange juice, pastries, barbary figs and *sfenj* (Moroccan doughnuts). In Tunisia you will find different specialities: *briks, fricassees* (puff pastries with flaked tuna) or the famous Tunisian sandwiches (rolls with *mechouia*, tinned tuna, *harissa* and capers).

A CUISINE
OF INFINITE VARIETY

The Maghrebi cuisine is full of surprises. The same ingredient may be used in many different ways in savoury or sweet dishes. Carrots can be cut into big chunks and added to a vegetable couscous; they can be sieved and mixed with almond paste to make delicious *petits fours*; grated and mixed with orange juice and orange-blossom water, they will make a refreshing salad; they can be steamed and seasoned with *harissa* and cumin to make a dish that will grace the *kemia* table; or they can be candied with sugar, spices and cinnamon to make a succulent candied fruit. Aubergines, broad beans, chick-peas, peppers, tomatoes, almond paste, semolina, dates and olives are equally versatile.

Maghrebi cuisine consists of an infinite range of savoury and sweet flavours and many contrasting styles of cooking. It is a cuisine where time does not seem to matter, where cooks take pleasure in choosing, washing, chopping and simmering ingredients, and filling the house with wonderful aromas.

YOUR EYE
IS YOUR SCALE

The *tabakhat* (cooks) never wrote down their recipes, instead recipes were passed down orally. Cooking was an art, an art that used all the senses to reach the right flavour, texture and colour without the bother of measuring. When one asked, 'How much of this?' or 'How much of that?' the usual answer was, 'Your eye is your scale.' So the result always reflected the mood of the cook: more or less salty, more or less sweet, more or less hot, more or less spicy or more or less bland.

Traditional Moroccan cooks, who work behind the scenes at a feast, are called *dadas*. They work bent over in a jack-knife position, instead of standing at a kitchen counter, or sometimes squatting if they are grinding something that requires force. The tools they use in a traditional Maghrebi kitchen are slightly different from the tools used in a Western kitchen. You will find a glossary of Maghrebi cooking equipment on page 219.

> We planted the word 'if': it sprouted the words 'Oh, I wish.'
>
> Arabic proverb

Clockwise from top left: market vendor in Morocco; shadow in Fez; tagines in the market; village shop outside Marrakech

HOSPITALITY AND MANNERS

To be a guest at a Moorish dinner party is somewhat trying to the uninitiated. There are no chairs, tables, knives, forks or spoons. The company sit in a circle, cross-legged, on the floor. Sometimes, indeed, an apology for a table, a few inches in height, is placed in the centre... before eating, everyone says grace for himself by exclaiming: Bismillah! In the name of God!

Arthur Leared, Morocco and the Moors, 1876

In the Maghreb, eating is an art form. It is customary to provide so much food that it would be impossible for any guest to finish it – dish after dish of spiced soups, smouldering *tagines*, bowls of spiced olives, roasted meats, vegetables, breads and sweets.

Here, there is a great philosophy of abundance, generosity, sharing, receiving and hospitality. 'You will open the door to any stranger' goes a North African proverb, 'And you will bestow your hospitality on him for three whole days before inquiring as to the object of his visit.' Even in the most humble homes, it would be unthinkable for someone to visit without being offered tea and sweet pastries fragrant with rose-petal and orange-blossom water.

Meals in North Africa are eaten in a manner that is very different from the West. In the Maghreb there is a different philosophy of the table. The most important thing to remember is to take one's time. There is a Maghrebi proverb: '*Celui qui n'a pas le temps est un homme mort*' ('He who has no time is dead'). This pertains not only to the preparation of the meal – which can take days if one is preparing for a *moussem* (a festival celebrating, for instance, a bountiful harvest) – but also to the actual time spent at the table eating. Pacing oneself is essential as the amount of food that is brought out is staggering.

As Louis Brunot, a French anthropologist who wrote *Au Seuil de la Vie Marocaine* observed earlier in this century:

Formal manners dictate that one must only use three fingers to eat: the thumb, the forefinger and the middle finger. Using only one finger speaks of the devil's influence, prophets eat with three, only gluttons eat with four or five. It is permissible, however, to eat food of a softer consistency with five fingers.

Once you get used to eating with your hands, it becomes difficult to do otherwise; it seems to enhance the flavour of the food because you can appreciate the texture so much more. The skill displayed by people who have eaten with their hands all their lives is astonishing; couscous is made into a little ball with the hand and fed with incomparable dexterity into the mouth.

'When you have guests, it is best to have a tagine,' says a Moroccan chef. 'It is beautiful to look at, you can cook other things while you are cooking it, and you can eat it with your hands, which makes the guests feel more at home with each other.'

One final note. One cannot really write a book about the North African table (or indeed, the Middle Eastern table), without mentioning burping. While it is seen as offensive in the West, it is seen as appreciative or even gracious here. After burping, one says 'Nhemdou Allah', meaning 'We praise God.'

'It is a way of thanking Allah for the opulent food and the wealth of spices and herbs used in the cooking,' says Rahil Abdel Jalil, from the *Herboriste du Paradis* in Marrakech.

> **The most delicious dish is. 'Fast and then eat.'**
> Arabic proverb

HOLIDAYS AND CELEBRATIONS

Muslim holidays and family celebrations all have their own special culinary traditions.

Ramadan is the ninth month of the Islamic calendar and commemorates the time when the Koran was revealed to the Prophet Mohammed. If you visit North Africa during *ramadan* it is important to be aware of the local customs. Most shops and restaurants are closed and for 29 or 30 days a strict fast is observed. This means no eating, drinking, smoking or sex from dawn to sunset. In Morocco, people are forbidden by law from 'public disrespect' of the fast.

For most people it is a time of reflection and purification. The days move slowly and quietly. But when the sun sets, things come alive; the streets and cafes become a different world. Most people break their fast with a soup, usually *harira*, and possibly a glass of milk or some dates. Algerians eat *chorba* soup with meat. This is usually followed by a long feast which can include several *tagines* and many platters of sweets. Lamb is popular during *ramadan*. On the fourteenth and twenty-seventh day of the fast, the principal dish served is either a chicken or a lamb couscous.

Aid El Fitr (also called *Aid el Seghir*) celebrates the end of *ramadan*. It takes place at the first sighting of the moon marking the beginning of the month of Choual. It is always a wild celebration and a time of great eating, giving and spending. Traditionally it is a time of giving grain, dates or money to the poor. Children are taken out shopping and bought new clothes, adults gather and see old friends, arriving at houses with heavy boxes of wrapped sweets. Delicious pastries appear on every family table.

Aid El Adha (also called *Aid el Kebir*). According to the Koran, the angel Gabriel came down from heaven and prevented Abraham from sacrificing his only son. This is commemorated by the sacrifice of a lamb. The sacrifice is done by the head of the family, reciting a prayer. Some of the hardier members of the family eat the liver raw, and in the evening, there is a special dish that varies from family to family, but which always involves eating the lamb's head.

Mouharam is the first day of the new year according to the Islamic moon-based calendar. This day also celebrates the *Hijra*, or the migration of the Prophet Mohammed from Mecca to Medina. In Algeria a dish of pasta with chicken *(rechta bel djedj)* is served.

El Mawlid Ennabaoui is a traditional and religious holiday that celebrates the birthday of the Prophet Mohammed. Couscous is the traditional dish served here.

Aid El Achoura is the tenth day of the first month of the year. Traditionally one gives one tenth of everything one has to the poorest. The day is celebrated with a dish of couscous with lamb or chicken.

Bedouins eating a couscous in the desert

THE LITTLE FINGERS OF THE BRIDE

Because Arabic and Berber are highly descriptive languages in which analogy and metaphor are used abundantly, many dishes have very evocative names. *Swibaat laaroussa* ('the little fingers of the bride') is an example. In North Africa brides are often very young and this expression is used to describe either delicate pastries with almonds or tiny tender courgettes. *Sakran tayah fi droudj* ('the drunkard falling down the stairs') describes a dish in which the most unexpected flavours collide with each other: orange-blossom water, vinegar, lemon, garlic, cinnamon, lamb, eggs and onion. *Khdoud Zouana* means 'Zouana's cheeks'; Zouana was a legendary fat man and this expression is used for eggy bread in a syrup of honey and orange-blossom water. *Merk hzina* ('widow's soup') is really a salad. Then there is *reza del Kadi*, ('*Kadi*'s turban'); *Kadi* means a judge and this is the name given to a rolled pastry in a turban shape. *Chbakiya* ('grid') is a cunningly woven, honeyed pastry which is eaten by both Muslims and Jews after a fast. *Kaab el ghzal* are pastries shaped in the form of gazelle horns. The famous *tagine del guezzar* ('butcher's *tagine*') is a dish of tripe, offal, oxtail and calf's foot – these are reckoned to be the choicest cuts reserved by the butcher for his family. (There's also *tagine del guezzar delmeskin* – 'poor man's butcher's *tagine*' – which contains only tripe.)

Lastly there is *tagine del sebbana* ('washerwoman's *tagine*') or *tagine del sebbagh* ('painter's *tagine*'). This dish might be white beans with *kefta* or a meat and vegetable stew put together with whatever vegetables are found in the house that day. It's a dish which may sound relatively elaborate today but which used to be reserved for days when there was no time for 'real' cooking – either washing days or days when the house was being painted. In past times walls were painted to half their height once a week, rather than being simply cleaned.

STORYTELLING, RECIPES AND THE ORAL TRADITION

In the Arab world storytelling is as ingrained in the culture as the love of good food – think of Scheherazade and *One Thousand and One Nights*. In the North African countryside people, often illiterate, would pass stories from one village to another. The professional storytellers that one finds for example in the Place Djemaa El Fna in Marrakech are not there simply to attract tourists. On the contrary the stories are told in Arabic and the attentive audience is made up of local people. Every storyteller is a talented actor. They narrate, they mime, they live out their stories with such realism that even those who do not understand the language cannot take their eyes away.

In North Africa, oral history is important. According to Henry Munson Jr, an American professor of anthropology who spent years recording the history of one family in Morocco (and who wrote the excellent book *The House of Si Abd Allah: The Oral History of a Moroccan Family*), oral traditions become microcosms, miniature social and cultural histories. 'Oral history inevitably reflects the social situation in which it is recorded,' he says.

Oral history includes family legends, sagas and also recipes. Traditions, legends and stories accompany certain dishes that every family hands down. 'We talk about everything, but very little is written down,' says Solange Azagury-Partridge, a well-known London jeweller of Moroccan-Jewish extraction. Indeed, her mother, a brilliant cook from Casablanca, does not write down the recipes, she talks about them and relays them to her daughter while she is cooking. So the *tagine de mouton* or the *skheena del'houmous ul loobia* (a traditional *dafina*) comes to the table along with storytelling.

> *A piece of bread and an onion with peace, is better than a stuffed lamb with quarrels.*
>
> Arabic proverb

THE STORY OF THE SHEEP'S EYE

Europeans mistakenly believe that the Maghrebis eat sheep's eyes. This apparently comes from an incident in which a party of diplomats was invited to a feast by their Arab host. They were shown the eye of the sheep that they were about to eat so that they could admire its clarity, signifying the freshness of the meat. Not wishing to offend their host, one of the diplomats swallowed it, assuming that he was being offered a delicacy. The Arab host, who had never eaten a sheep's eye in his life, assumed that it was a delicacy in the west and served them to his European guests thereafter. Whether or not this story is apocryphal, it is nevertheless told throughout North Africa.

Herbs,

Herbs and spices are essential to all Middle Eastern cooking and in the Maghreb they are paramount. The love and reverence that is paid to spices comes from the region's history. Boxes and jars of mysterious, colourful powder were first brought by Phoenicians and were treasured like gold. Long before modern medicine most herbs and spices were known for their medicinal uses. To this day each spice merchant has his own tricks and recipes and knows which substance will get rid of the evil eye, cure a headache or increase fertility.

Spices

& other ingredients

HERBS, SPICES AND OTHER INGREDIENTS

I have a memory: it is Wednesday lunchtime in a cupboard-size nameless restaurant in the Marrakech *souk*. It is the day of the weekly cattle market, when farmers and restaurateurs gather in the misty light to barter animals. Mark (the photographer of this book) and I have been brought to the *souk* by Ahmed Benbadryef, a friend who owns an amazing lantern shop that is stuffed fuller than Aladdin's cave. He tells us that we will taste the best *brochettes* in all of Marrakech, perhaps in Morocco. Early that morning the elderly proprietor has bought fresh beef, lamb and chicken, which he is moulding into patties or *brochettes* behind a small counter. He uses his hands, kneading the meat and mixing it with a spoonful of green olive oil that he keeps in a soda bottle under the counter. He adds garlic and a handful of bronze-coloured spices called *ras-el-hanout* ('head of the shop'). When he is convinced the mixture is perfect, he rolls it onto a stick and places the *brochettes* on a flame, where they are roasted slowly, sealing in the juices. When the meat has finished cooking, the sticks are piled high on a plain dish and served along with a simple salad of lettuce and tomatoes, a small dish of cracked,

spiced olives and chunks of warm brown bread which the old man has ripped apart with his hands. We eat quickly, barely looking up. But when I do, I see men sitting two or three to a table, all eating off the same plate with looks of sheer indulgence on their faces. It is a simply prepared dish, but nothing short of art.

I have another memory: in a beautiful house in the countryside outside of Marrakech, waking to a bath with lavender water which has been poured from large jars; followed by a breakfast on a verandah of hot, fresh bread and eggs scrambled with cumin. The smell of lavender follows me all day.

Or a final memory: an enormous meal at the Restaurant *Saveurs de Poissons*, a tiny local restaurant hidden in an alleyway in Tangier, which serves, at the end of the long meal, a home-made tisane brewed from thyme, rosemary and bee pollen. This potion, believes Mohammed Belhadj, the owner, is an essential ingredient for keeping alive.

Clockwise from top left: mint tea; street food vendors; spices; spice merchant in Tunis central market

SHOPPING IN NORTH AFRICA

In Morocco, particularly in the *souks* or *mellahs* (Jewish districts), different kinds of shops were gathered together in whole streets. All the jewellery stores (*dhaibiya*) occupied one street, the embroidery stores (*fondouk*) were in another street and the spice and herb merchants (*aatarine*) sold herbal treatments and spice mixes in a third street.

Most North African recipes call for a number of spices, herbs, fragrant waters, sauces and other ingredients which are vital to the recipe's success and not interchangeable. All of these can be found in Britain in large supermarkets or in specialist stores.

Boys returning home in the morning with *sfenj* (doughnuts) for the family

A GLOSSARY OF NORTH AFRICAN INGREDIENTS

Absinthe *(chiba)* A thin-leaved, light green/grey herb with a bitter taste, used fresh or dried, alone or with fresh mint to make tea.

Ale or Illan A green grain, the size of a peppercorn. A soup made with *ale* and served with dates and bread is supposed to strengthen the bones.

Alum *(chebb)* Ground and used in *jabane* – a soft nougat with nuts or almonds. Alum is burnt with *hermel*, (a fragrant spice) and *houd* (sandalwood) in a little *kanoun* (an earthenware brazier) in order to counteract the evil eye.

Aniseed *(nafaa or hlaouoa enafaa)* Used in bread, pastries and cookies.

Ash berries *(lissan ettir)* These are ground and used in certain *ras-el-hanout* blends.

Basil *(hbeq)* Basil is hardly ever used in traditional North African cuisine. Instead it is valued for its medicinal virtues. It is good to fight stress and insomnia, and it is used alone or with mint to make a tisane. Placed around the house it will ward off insects.

Bay leaf *(ouarka sidna moussa)* The leaves are used fresh or dried in a bouquet garni.

Black pepper *(ibzar el'khel)* Used finely ground or as whole peppers in pickled vegetables or pickled meats. Black pepper is better kept whole and crushed as needed. In our recipes we recommend white pepper instead of black pepper.

Cantharis or Spanish fly *(debbant el hend)* A ground insect used in *ras-el-hanout*.

Caraway seeds *(kerouiya)* Caraway aids digestion. Tunisians rely heavily upon this spice to flavour *harissa*.

Cardamom *(gagulla)* Used ground in *ras-el-hanout* and occasionally to flavour coffee. Cardamom aids respiratory problems.

Cayenne pepper *(felfla soudaniya)* Very small, very hot dried red chilli peppers. Used either whole or crushed.

Celery *(krafss)* Used in *harira*.

Cinnamon *(kerfa or dar el cini)* There are two kinds of cinnamon: *dar el cini* is the delicate version from Sri Lanka; *kerfa* is usually from Vietnam and has a stronger taste. It is used ground or whole, in sweet lamb or duck dishes, in drinks and in candied fruits. Ground cinnamon, mixed with icing sugar, is used to flavour *pastilla* and some sweet couscous, such as couscous *seffa*. Cinnamon is often sprinkled over a dish. It is a powerful bactericide. An infusion of cinnamon sticks and cloves can help fight the flu.

Cloves *(oud el'kronfel)* Used ground or whole, in *tagines*, fruit salads or candied fruits with spices. Also used to pickle meat. Chewing a clove is supposed to relieve toothache and prevent bad breath. Cloves also have digestive and antiseptic properties and stimulate physical and intellectual activity.

Coriander *(kasbour)* Coriander is normally used fresh in North African cuisine. The seeds are used to flavour pickled meats and occasionally in cooking. Coriander is mentioned as an aphrodisiac in the *One Thousand and One Nights*. Coriander alleviates urinary infections.

Cubeb pepper *(nouioura)* Part of the spice mixture used for meatballs.

Cumin *(kamoun)* Cumin seeds are toasted and ground, and used with grilled meats (*brochettes* and *keftas*) or chicken livers. Cumin is a very important ingredient of *chermoula* sauce, used to marinate fish or meat. Cumin is added to salads of cooked vegetables, such as aubergines, carrots, beetroots, swiss chard, and broad beans. Cumin is known to ease digestion. In some Jewish families, ground cumin used to be given to young children with a teaspoon of *mahia* (a distilled liquor of figs and aniseed) to relieve stomach ache.

Felfla harra Ground dried red hot peppers.

Felfla hloua Sweet dried red peppers.

Fennel *(besbass)* Fennel has a distinctive smell rather like aniseed. The whole bulb is used as a vegetable with meat (page 160) or in mixed pickled vegetables with lemon. The feathery fronds are used in fish marinades. Fennel is good to ease kidney pains.

Fenugreek *(halba)* Used in couscous *del'Hsoub* (page 121) which is reputed to be an aphrodisiac. Fenugreek is also an expectorant.

Garlic *(toum)* Garlic is a major ingredient in North African cooking. It cures worms in children and is used as an antiseptic.

Ginger *(skinjbir)* Except for certain, more modern North African recipes, ginger is usually used dried and ground, not as grated fresh root. In some fish, meat or poultry recipes ginger marries very successfully with saffron. It is also used in drinks, pastries and candied fruits and vegetables, such as candied baby aubergines. Ginger is known as an aphrodisiac, and an infusion of ginger can help stomach disorders.

Green tea *(atai)* Mint tea is always made with green tea. The most commonly used is gunpowder tea. Green tea is a diuretic and an astringent for the fibres of the stomach, toning it and improving digestion.

Gum arabic *(meska)* Used ground in candied aubergines or in *jabane*, a soft nougat with nuts or almonds. Also used in coffee.

Hebdi A deep green mint. Used alone or with other varieties of mint to make mint tea.

Herch A variety of mint with rough leaves. Used alone or with other varieties of mint to make mint tea.

Juniper *(nowera)* Used ground. Part of the spices *El'Hsoub*. Juniper is famous for encouraging the appetite. The berries are also reputed to give pregnant women a speedy delivery.

Mace *(mashia or bsibsa)* Mace is the orange outer casing of the nutmeg. It has a strong perfume, and is used ground, particularly to flavour meatballs or fish balls.

Nutmeg *(gouza or gouzt ettib or gouza belloutiya)* Nutmeg should be used freshly grated. Nutmeg and cinnamon are usually an excellent combination in fruit salads, candied fruits, pastries and in certain sweet *tagines* with spices. Nutmeg and mace used to be used in hypnotic and calming medications. Nutmeg is also a good general antiseptic.

Olives *(zitoun)* Olives are always pickled or salted. There are many different varieties: black wrinkled salty olives, large purple olives pickled in lemon, green olives pickled in lemon with garlic, and black or green olives in *chermoula* sauce. They are eaten as an appetiser or included in salads. Cracked green olives with a slightly bitter taste are cooked with lamb, beef, chicken and fish.

Onions *(besla)* An Arab proverb says: *Once you reach a new country, eat of its onions.* There is a widespread belief that when one eats onions in a new country, one becomes immune to colds or stomach upsets. Onions also increase male fertility, and the juice of onions is good for burns.

Oregano *(zaatar)* Oregano is infused in hot water to make a strong, bitter herbal tea to relieve tummy aches and digestion problems.

Paprika *(felfla hloua)* Paprika comes in various shades of crimson and orange. Used ground in cooked salads (of aubergines, carrots, beetroot and swiss chard). It combines very well with cumin in fish dishes or in *brochettes* and *keftas*. It is used to make red sauce and *chermoula* sauce.

Parsley *(maadnous)* Generous quantities of flat-leaved parsley are used in lots of North African dishes (the curly-leaved variety is very rare). It is sold in large bunches. In our recipes we have translated one bunch into six tablespoons of chopped fresh parsley (and we've done the same for fresh coriander). Parsley is extremely rich in vitamin C. Lay the leaves on the eyes to reduce inflammation.

Peppermint *(naana ikama)* The most common variety of mint. It is used alone or with other varieties of mint to make mint tea. Sprigs of mint are used to decorate *pastilla* and orange salad with orange-blossom water and cinnamon. At the entrance of the tanners' *souk* in Fez, a sprig of fresh mint is given to all the visitors in order to hide the overpowering smell of the *souk*. Mint has tonic and stimulating virtues, and therefore should be avoided before going to sleep. It is useful for all disorders of the stomach, including weakness, loss of appetite, pain and vomiting.

Pickled lemon *(hamad mraquade)* A basic ingredient in Moroccan cooking and very easy to make at home (page 141). It can also be bought from shops. Pickled lemons are used in *tagines* and in cooked or raw salads. Pickled lemons are very salty, so always reduce the quantity of salt in recipes that contain them.

Pine kernels or pine nuts Toasted pine kernels are sprinkled over some lamb or chicken *tagines*. Tunisians use them to add flavour and texture to their mint tea.

Ras-el-hanout Literally 'head of the shop'. The meaning is the 'crème de la crème' of the shop. *Ras-el-hanout* can be bought ready made. It is a blend of aromatic powdered spices, herbs and roots that is used in certain *tagines* or couscous. Here is one of the many recipes for *ras-el-hanout*: $^1/_2$ teaspoon ground turmeric, $^1/_2$ teaspoon ground ginger, $^1/_2$ teaspoon ground mace, $^1/_2$ teaspoon ground maniguette (a sort of nutmeg from the Sahara, called *gouza sahraouia* in Arabic), $^1/_2$ teaspoon grated nutmeg, $^1/_2$ teaspoon ground cardamom, $^1/_2$ teaspoon paprika, $^1/_2$ teaspoon ground black pepper, $^1/_2$ teaspoon ground ash bay, $^1/_2$ teaspoon ground cinnamon, $^1/_2$ teaspoon cantharis (optional). Depending on the whims of the spice merchant, *ras-el-hanout* may include up to a hundred ingredients. Each shopkeeper has his own secret recipe and his own claims as to the blend's medicinal power.

Saffron *(zaafran)* Saffron is the noblest spice. It gives dishes a unique taste and a wonderful golden yellow colour. The ancient Pharaohs believed that saffron had supernatural properties and anointed honoured guests with its oil. Saffron is also very expensive. It takes 75,000 hand-picked crocuses to make one pound of saffron.
To make the best use of saffron, grind the strands into a fine powder with a pestle and mortar. This can then be infused and the infusion used in recipes (see page 68). Some recipes may require you to use the strands whole, but generally this doesn't give a good distribution of the aroma, taste and colour. Saffron should always be bought as strands, not powder, particularly in the Moroccan *souks*. Otherwise there is a danger you will be buying false saffron (*cartham*), which is just a colouring powder. *Zaafran beldi* – a word that comes from *bled*, 'the village' – is the authentic saffron. Saffron refreshes the spirits and is good against fainting fits and palpitations of the heart.

Sage *(salmiya)* Used with other herbs in a bouquet garni, or crushed and kneaded into dough to make a special bread, *khobz salmiya*. Sage stops bleeding and can be used to cleanse sores.

Sesame seeds *(jeljlane)* North Africans use sesame seeds whole, and they always toast them. Sesame seeds are used in breads and pastries, and to make a nougat, *haloua del'jeljlane*. They are often used as a garnish – mainly in sweet *tagines*. To the Jews sesame seeds are a symbol of prosperity and are part of the *Rosh Hashana* table (Jewish New Year).

Smen This is rancid butter and it is traditionally used in certain meat dishes or couscous. It is made with salted butter which is melted and strained. *Smen*, which is similar to clarified butter, has a very strong taste, so in our recipes we have used sunflower oil or unsalted butter instead.

Soffi A downy green-grey mint. Used alone or with other varieties of mint to make mint tea.

Sugar *(s'kkor)* North Africans have a well-deserved reputation for having a very sweet palate. Their cuisine includes a huge variety of small pastries. Most are dipped in a sugar syrup flavoured with orange-blossom water, lemon zest or vanilla. Mint tea is usually very sweet – it is sweetened with sugar chipped from large loaves. Sugar is included in a wide range of sweet *tagines*.

Sweet marjoram *(merdeddouche)* Used alone or with other varieties of mint to make mint tea. Sweet marjoram warms and comforts head colds.

Thyme *(z'iitra)* This is used either fresh or dried. It combines very well with coriander. Thyme is a powerful bactericide and is used to treat external and internal infections.

Turmeric or curcuma *(kherkoum)* Always used ground. Turmeric is a deep yellow powder with a light taste but a strong colour. It's much cheaper than saffron and can replace it in most recipes. Turmeric is therefore called 'the saffron of the poor'.

Vervain *(louisa)* Used alone or with other varieties of mint to make mint tea. Vervain helps soothe coughs.

Watermelon rind This is used to make candied peel.
There is a proverb which says: 'He cures fever with watermelon rind'. In other words his remedies don't last long; watermelon rind is placed on the foreheads of people suffering from high fever, but the relief it gives is only temporary.

White pepper *(ibzar el'byed)* Used ground. White pepper has a stronger flavour than black pepper and should therefore be used carefully. In our recipes, we prefer white pepper to black pepper for aesthetic reasons.

Wild mint *(fliou)* Fliou has a wonderful strong fragrance. It is used alone or with other varieties of mint to make mint tea. Dried *fliou*, put in a little cloth purse and sniffed, treats a cold.

HENNA

Henna is believed to have been Mohammed's favourite plant. One of the most important cosmetic rituals in Morocco is the application of henna in elaborate patterns. The night before a wedding, it is customary for a bride and her friends to receive a visit from the *neqqachat*. These are women skilled in the application of henna to the feet, hands and face.

Henna can also be used to enhance hair thickness and colour. It gives a warm reddish glow to brown hair. But beware, the longer henna is left on, the redder it becomes.

A bride may be in the process of being dressed for her wedding and yet she knows not who shall marry her.

Arabic proverb

This is one recipe which comes from a *neqqachat* in old Tangier: mix one-quarter of a cup of henna powder with a pinch of ground cloves and three-quarters of a cup of water in a pan. Bring to a boil and simmer ten minutes; let it cool and apply to the hair. Let the mixture dry all day – the head will become very heavy. For more body, add an egg or a teaspoon of olive oil. An application left for more than one hour lasts six to eight weeks.

But perhaps the most notorious henna ritual is that of the ancient Berber women who were believed to be the Amazons of Diodorus Siculus. They were renowned for leading their men into war and they hennaed any man who showed his cowardice.

FRAGRANT WATERS

The North Africans use orange-blossom water and rose-petal water to flavour cakes, *tagines* and salads but, even more important than their culinary uses, fragrant waters are widely used in beauty preparations. In Morocco, where people eat with their hands, it is traditional to wash your hands both before and after the meal in water perfumed with orange-blossom or rose-petal water.

Clockwise from top left: two women in *djellabas*; rose petals in fountain; hennaed hands; Moroccan garden viewed through a screen

The distilling process was invented by the Arabs centuries ago. It takes seven pounds of rosebuds or orange blossoms to make one gallon of fragrant water.

Orange-blossom water (*ma zhar*) Orange-blossom water is made from a distillation of orange-flower blossoms. It is used in salads, in candied fruits, or in drinks. Orange-blossom water combines very well with cinnamon.

It is very famous for its calming virtue; mixed into hot milk with sugar it is recommended in cases of insomnia.

Rose-petal water (*ma ouard*) Rose-petal water is made from distilled rose petals and used either as a perfume or to flavour pastries or desserts, like the rose-petal water *tabbouleh* with fresh fruit. It can be found in any North African souk and is one of the most useful and potent beauty products that a woman can find. According to the Berbers, who are renowned for their fine-textured skin, rose-petal water should be applied morning and night after washing the face. Not only does the scent clear the senses (the scent of dried roses is a well-known antidepressant), but the water refreshes and moisturises the skin. According to Myriem, the hennaed woman who sold me bottles of fresh rose-petal water: 'des pétales de roses pour lutter contre la fatigue et de la marjolaine pour délivrer de l'anxiété'. (Rose petals to combat fatigue and marjoram to relieve stress and anxiety.)

> **He who eats honey must expect the bee sting.**
> Arabic proverb

Rahil Abdel Jalil, who works in *Herboriste du Paradis* on the Place Ben Youssef in Marrakech says that rose-petal water is also good to add to hair as a final rinse ('it prevents hair loss') or add one drop to mint tea to combat depression.

Morocco is a great producer of roses. Outside Marrakech, where roses are farmed specifically for this purpose, one can find greenhouses full of deep crimson and aubergine-coloured roses, the petals of which are gathered, bundled and then pressed into water. In Morocco fresh rose petals are scattered over the tablecloth to decorate the table, or scattered over the water in the fountains of the beautiful *riyad* patios. Dried rosebuds are used as pot-pourri in large ceramic bowls or they are crushed and added to certain spice mixtures, such as the spices used for meatballs.

Lavender water (*khzama helhal*) Another important fragrant water.

Dried lavender is used in drinks, breads, pastries and desserts, and also as part of *ras-el-hanout*. Lavender is of special use for pains in the head following a cold.

The fragrance of lavender has a soothing, healing effect. Oil of lavender can be added to washing and, when burned, it acts as a powerful aid against insomnia. 'It also protects against moths', says Abdel Jalil, 'and can be used as an antiseptic after a woman has a baby.'

Seller of fragrant waters in Tunis

OIL

We have come to Tamesloht, an oil-producing village outside of Marrakech, at sunset. People walk slowly home from the village water pump where they have come to fill their buckets. The dying sun has turned the colours of the houses to a pinky stone colour. Children play in the street, waiting for the evening meal to begin.

On the outskirts, Abdullah Jinjie, 46 years old, is finishing his day. He owns a small olive press; his son works beside him and he learned his trade from his father. He was ten when he began working with olive oil. He collected olives from the tree and brought them home in baskets to his father. When he was older, '[my father] found me a wife and the wife got me a child.' Then his father died and the olive oil press – an ancient device consisting of a gigantic wheel with a mule pulling it – became his.

After the mule and the wheel squeeze the oil, it is strained in an underground cave with a rope. It is an archaic process; one wonders if it is just handed down from generation to generation without any logic, but the end result is a heavy, green, delicious oil which is unlike the oils of the Mediterranean that I am used to.

Abdullah Jinjie produces 200 litres in three days and the season runs for four to five months beginning in October, when the olives are gathered from under the trees, and ending in February, when the green oil is bottled and sold to the market. After February, Abdullah Jinjie begins to think of trading, mainly in the south. 'Everything I do involves olive oil,' he says. 'If I did not have olive oil, I would not be here.'

His life is contained and small. There is a wonderful sense of continuation to his routine. Does he ever get bored, or wonder about the world outside of his village? He ponders this, scratching his beard. 'Sometimes I try to sell olive oil to the people of the Sahara,' he says. 'Once I stayed twelve days. It took me one day through the Atlas mountains in a beautiful new Mercedes belonging to a friend. But when I arrived there was already olive oil in the Sahara.' So he turned back and came home. 'I have enough people to sell to here,' he said.

North African olive oil is thick with a deep green colour. It is kept for special salads or preserves, such as dried red peppers in olive oil. One of the best ways to eat it is with freshly baked bread for breakfast, though in poor families bread and olive oil may replace any meal. Large tablespoons of olive oil used to be given to weak children to make them stronger.

HONEY (ASSEL)

I was lost in the *medina* of Fez in the twisting, wandering alleys somewhere near the Zaouia of Moulay Idriss II, one of the holiest buildings in the city. I took a lucky turn and found the honey man. The honey man was called Abdul Abdel Arafaman and he stood in an open courtyard surrounded by metal vats of honey that reached to my waist.

It was a cold, rainy day. The honey man was drinking mint tea and rubbing his hands together to stay warm. He took several wooden spoons from a jar and began to dip them into the vats, giving me samples of every one. I was surprised to find that each honey had a different, unique taste.

The ways of the bees and the properties of honey Abdul Abdel was a happy man. He loved his work and was devoted to his bees. The honey, he said, was his life. He had been taught the ways of the bees since he was a small child growing up in the countryside outside of Fez and he knew by tasting a small spoonful of honey exactly what the bees had been feeding on. The domesticated bees that lived in boxes, he said, gave the weakest flavour. He said that he usually bought his honey from different Berber tribes who each had unique bees. There is, for instance, a honey made from bees who only suckle lavender. This honey, according to Abdul Abdel, is best for women with hormonal imbalances, mood swings and digestive problems.

Zaatar honey is made from bees who feast on the *Zaatar* flower which grows in the countryside. It is best used when one has a cold or respiratory problems.

Millefleur – the honey of 1,000 flowers – is the richest and sweetest. And finally *jbal*, which takes its name from a road leading to Ketama al Hosiama, a small village in the nearby mountains, is a honey made from bees who only eat figs.

'The Berbers always serve figs after a meal', says Abdul Abdel, 'not only because of their digestive properties, but because of the sweetness and delicacy of the fruit. When the bees eat only this fruit, the honey becomes a gift. It is so delicious that you only use it in small, special doses.'

The world was sharp under the sunlight. In Tangier, they had told me that I was mad to come here so late in the season. 'It will be a furnace,' they said. But it isn't. Not yet, in any case. The air was soft and limpid. The plain of Marrakech lay flat into the distance and beyond it the horseshoe of the High Atlas, snow still lying on the peaks. Everything was brilliantly defined – the mountains, the plain, the immense palm groves beyond the city walls, the city itself, gardens within the city, flat roofs round me in a complex of horizontal planes pierced with minarets.

Peter Mayne, *A Year in Marrakech*, 1953

Morocco

ARRIVAL IN MOROCCO

The name for Morocco in Arabic is *Jeziret al Maghreb*, 'the Isle of the Setting Sun'. Of all the North African countries, Morocco is the most modern but, paradoxically, it is also the most ancient. Because of this it's bewitching: it is impossible to arrive and not to find oneself mesmerised on some level. Morocco conjures up the most seductive and powerful images with just a smell or a glance: the crowded, vibrant *souk* packed with every variety of humanity; the rows of majestic palms; the pink-washed colour of the houses late in evening; the smell of cinnamon, cardamom and cloves.

We arrived late in Marrakech on an autumn night. The air was still heavy with summer, and perfumed. From the airport road, I could see the dark outline of the mountains and closer, the vast minaret of the twelfth-century Koutoubia. We drove through the Djemaa el Fna. It was nearly midnight, but the square was packed with *personnages*: snake charmers, jugglers, storytellers, water sellers in their traditional costumes, food vendors and tourists. We drove on to another smaller square, parked our car and then entered a labyrinth that led to our house.

> He hides himself in the shadow of his finger.
>
> Arabic proverb

Once you stepped in, there was a lush courtyard with a fountain; upstairs were four bedrooms overlooking it. Mine was long and narrow and the bed was a Spanish four-poster. There were mosaic tiles on the floor in the shape of stars and a vast walnut armoire. Every inch of the room – and the house – was filled with something beautiful to look at. It was a small house, but it was beautifully crafted and rich with colour, smells and life. It was a microcosm of Marrakech.

In the morning I woke to the sound of donkeys straining under the weight of their carts. My room was windowless, so I ran – still in my nightgown – up the stairs to the roof terrace. From it, I could see the street below me and the people moving slowly like ants: children carrying the day's bread on trays on their heads; veiled women on their way to the *hammam*. I could smell the bread from the communal bakery mixed with the coffee brewing downstairs. The sky was intensely blue; already it was very hot. I went down to breakfast. It was laid out with croissants that had been baked that morning; long stick-like *baguettes*; big cups of *café au lait*; sweet, thick honey from the souk; yoghurt made at home from soured milk; and two kinds of *confiture*, peach and strawberry.

Mosque in Fez

THE FOOD OF MOROCCO

The food of Morocco reflects its complicated history. All the different peoples who have settled here have made their mark upon the cuisine. From the Berbers come the *tagine* and *harira*; from the Arab Bedouins dates, milk, grains and bread; from the Moors olive oil, almonds, fruits and herbs; and from the Arabs spices from the islands of the Indian ocean and beyond.

According to some of the great food experts, the further south one travels in Morocco, the more African influence one sees. In Marrakech, the door of the desert, one might eat Khodra couscous with seven vegetables (the vegetables depend on whatever the cook finds that day in the market), or in the summer, *zaalouk*, which is made from aubergines. The further north one travels, Spanish cuisine becomes more influential.

Respect is given to wealth, not to men.
Arabic proverb

MARRAKECH

We stayed first in Marrakech which, along with Fez, is one of the great culinary centres of Morocco. It was here that I learned the philosophies of the Moroccan table, in particular the importance of taking one's time.

We spent Yom Kippur in Marrakech, and ate at the home of a Jewish friend. Sitting in her open-air courtyard, around a small table, we shared plates of *quare lahem bil jelbana* (meatballs in a clear sauce) from a family recipe; salads of green beans; salad *mechouia*; a salad of green peppers softened with *argan* oil, which has a distinctive, sharp taste; and lamb chops grilled on the flame.

Left and right: salt merchant pouring mint tea in the central market in Marrakech

TANGIER

Rich in prototypal dream scenes: covered streets like corridors with doors opening into rooms on either side, hidden terraces high above the sea, streets consisting only of steps, dark impasses, small squares built on sloping terrain so that they looked like ballet sets designed in false perspective, with alleys leading off in several different directions; as well as the classical dream equipment of tunnels, ramparts, ruins, dungeons and cliffs.

Paul Bowles

Tangier is a port city, a place that straddles the Atlantic Ocean on one side and the Straits of Gibraltar on the other. That alone makes it a romantic place. To me, all port cities have the same allure: the pungent smell of the sea; the influx of displaced people waiting to be somewhere else; the seedy, slightly threatening cafes, the dark winding streets at night filled with promises, surprises, dreams. When one is in Tangier, one cannot help but have a sense of journey. There are maybe three or four places in the world that have that kind of evocative quality – Marseille, for instance, Abidjan, or Split. One feels excited just sitting in a cafe sipping mint tea, as though anything could happen. And it does,

because these kinds of places are full of life's characters. Tangier, without a doubt, is one of those places.

We stayed in the *medina*, at the Hotel Continental. The hotel was built in 1865 and Queen Victoria's son Alfred was its first official guest. My room had a small window which opened onto the port, and further out from the sea, at the horizon, there was a full, heavy moon, so clear and close it looked as though I could touch it. Next to it was Venus, burning so brightly in the sky that it looked as though it could catch fire. Nothing could possibly go wrong in a city that had that kind of ambience.

Once an 'international zone' with its own laws and administration, it is full of magic: a hypnotic, dreamy kind of magic. There is a charm to the heady mixture of cultures which is reflected in the food: Andalucian at the Cafe Haffa – an outdoor tea garden from the 1920s that is carved into the cliffs overlooking the harbour – our mobile telephones picked up Spanish networks; Berber; French; African; even Central European (there was a large community of refugees here after World War II).

Eclectic dishes Now, there are even more eclectic mixtures of food. The food writer Paula Wolfert, who lived in Tangier for nearly 20 years until 1976, recently returned for the first time and was startled to find many things had changed, most of all the food. She discovered that the dish of the moment was an odd concoction: 'an ersatz *pastilla* filled with Moroccan spiced fish and Chinese noodles! Claudio served me a version – small crisp rolls stuffed with gelatinous pasta and coriander-scented shrimp. Then we got more traditional, with a delicious lamb, okra and quince *tagine*.'

Fish in Morocco Despite the fact that one side of the country borders the Atlantic, Moroccans are not great fish eaters. Although Morocco produces and exports a great deal of fish – particularly its famous tinned sardines – historically fish travelled badly and there was the problem of how to keep it. Moroccans, unlike the Spanish or the Italians, do not eat dried fish. Food expert, Abderrahim Bargache, has one of Morocco's most popular television shows, *Walima*. 'North African culture is not really a water culture,' he says. 'We trade goods and ideas across the lands, not across the sea. Traditionally we are meat eaters. We eat a lot of lamb. In the south, people like to eat camels. Fish is thought to be insulting to serve guests: in small villages in the countryside, when family visits family, it is traditional to stay at least three days. When the host wants to signify that it is time for the guest to go, he will serve a fish.'

> *I salute you with a box filled with sesame seeds. Each seed represents one hundred greetings.*
>
> Arabic proverb

TWO MEALS IN TANGIER

The first day in Tangier, we ate lunch in a local restaurant down the steps from the famous hotel El Minzah. The restaurant was run by a highly energetic man called Mohammed Belhadj who seated us at one of the six long wooden tables and, without taking our order, proceeded to bring out dish after dish of local specialities, many of which he could not name. The three chefs worked in an open kitchen with a charcoal grill and cooked using whatever ingredients they found at the market and the harbour that day. 'Here you do not order,' Mohammed said. 'It is brought.'

I ate more than I have ever eaten in my entire life. We started out with *tapas* and thick brown bread with bowls of fat green olives. Then we had a heavy fish soup with crevettes. This was followed by condiments – roasted almonds and walnuts and *harissa*. With this, we were served a herbal drink of thyme, rosemary, bee pollen and honey, which Mohammed told us was 'to aid digestion'. We continued with a dish of crispy fried whitebait served with a platter of pickled vegetables; a fat, grilled white fish coated in herbs and stuffed with small shrimp with a blackened skin that everyone ate with their fingers; and a sizzling terracotta platter of calamari, egg, mussels, potatoes and white fish that everyone ate with chunks of bread. The latter is the traditional Tangier dish of *tagra*.

The first cake on the planet Dessert was a revelation: a mixture of barley and walnuts covered with dark brown honey. 'This,' claimed Mohammed 'was the first cake on the planet. When the first man arrived on this earth, he wanted something sweet. So he took the shaft of wheat, crushed the nuts and poured honey on top.' All of this, naturally, was followed by mint tea, so sweet that it made the teeth ache.

And the meal still had not ended. Mohammed arrived with plates of figs, split open to reveal their lush innards: on top was poured honey and the fruit was sprinkled with walnuts. 'In the Berber lands,' he said, 'you always eat figs after a meal to prevent indigestion.' Not wanting that, we ate every one on the plate.

Six musicians That night, we ate couscous in Restaurant Hamadi, which has been owned by the Zerioish family since the 1930s. There are red velvet walls and plush booths with embroidered cushions. Six musicians played for us; men who have known each other since they were teenagers from a small village outside of Tangier. Between songs they sat cross-legged on the platform and stared at us as though we were a television set presumably because they have been playing together every night in this restaurant for the past forty years and no longer have anything to say to each other. 'They came one night forty years ago,' says Farid, the current proprietor, who was not even born when they arrived. 'My father told me they had played at weddings and feasts in the mountains where they come from. They arrived here one night and never left.'

Musicians in Tangier

CASABLANCA

Casablanca, which was modelled after Marseille, is the largest port of the Maghreb and the principal Moroccan city in all but administration. It is a modern city. Young girls stroll in bikinis near Ain Diab; teenage boys with shaved heads and surfing t-shirts play football. In the beach cafes, there is a languid, cafe-society feeling.

Casablanca also has the largest Jewish community in Morocco. It is estimated that more than 60 per cent of Morocco's 6,000–7,000 Jews live here, mainly in the Lusitania and Anfa districts. While the Jewish population may seem relatively small in comparison to the overall population, their influence, particularly gastronomically, is vast. It is estimated that half the recipes in Morocco are of Jewish origin.

RABAT

Rabat is the seat of the Royal Family. Here is where young girls come to study in Rabat's Royal Cooking School. 1,500 girls apply; only 40 are taken to be trained to cook in the Palaces of the Royal Family.

The school is run by Aicha El Hamiani; 'Food is something that Moroccan girls learn from their mothers,' she says, 'So it is not something that is seen as real work. In the old days, the *dada* (the cook) did all the cooking. Now that is changed. When these girls arrived, they knew from their mothers how to cook, but what I feel is important to teach them is the motivation to preserve our cooking.'

We ate lunch at the school, in a vast dining room with plush lavender and gold silk banquettes. Plate after plate was brought; the meal lasted for two hours, but then Aicha has a disdain for what she calls '*la cuisine plus rapide*'. 'Normally, for a simple meal, we serve two or three entrées, several salads and a dessert', she says, passing around the steaming dish of *pastilla*. 'But you must know your guests. The important thing is that nothing is wasted. Most dishes, in fact, taste better the next day.'

Aside from the *pastilla*, we ate two *tagines*: one of lamb, prunes, apricots and dates; one with chicken and preserved lemons; then salads, breads and preserves, and desserts: the snowy gazelle horns and almond cakes. All of this was followed by mint tea while Aicha philosophised about the evolution of the Moroccan diet. 'The criteria of beauty in this country has changed,' she said mournfully.

'At the beginning of the century, it was a voluptuousness that was desired, and they used to say, "That woman is so beautiful, there is no Moroccan door big enough for her to enter."' She sighed and passed around the plate of sweets: 'The hungrier one was, the better. Now, unfortunately, we are following Europe; everything lighter, everything less.'

F E Z

It was rainy and cold when we arrived in Fez, the most ancient of the Imperial cities. The air seemed heavy, autumnal. The famous minarets of the city seemed shrouded in fog and even the *adhan*, the call to prayer (a sound that I find utterly comforting) seemed hoarse and croaky. 'Quince weather', I thought, remembering what an old Moroccan cook had told me: 'When you see quinces in the market, you know that the summer is over and that the winter has arrived.' It is this kind of weather that makes one yearn for heavier, more warming food.

Early in the morning, I woke to the rain outside my window and walked alone to the Fez El Bali, the old city. There I met a young boy my own age who looked ten years older. He was a teacher, but tried to earn money as an unofficial guide. Together, we wandered the *souk*: to the honey man with his barrels of the stuff in deeper and darker shades of gold; through the dyers' market with its heady, almost too-strong smell; and at last through the vegetable and spice market where I saw that indeed the selection of vegetables had changed.

In the spice stalls I bought a dried chameleon to throw in my fireplace back in England to ward off the evil eye; a handful of dried lavender for my cupboards to protect my clothes from moths; and some orange-blossom water to use on my salads. The old man who sold me the goods opened the plastic bottle for me and stuck it under my nose: I closed my eyes and I was not, at that moment, in a crowded, cold *souk* with rain dripping on my head: I was in the midst of an orange grove in the South, somewhere near the desert. When I opened my eyes, the man was smiling. I bought the bottle.

At the meat market, I saw extraordinary things: sheep's heads with the eyes still glazed and milky; pink, runny hearts; tripe hanging over the edge of the counter; enormous slabs of liver.

tomato confit
with golden sesame seeds

Modern recipe:

SERVES 6 AS A SALAD OR STARTER

75 g (2³/4 oz) sesame seeds

8 large, ripe tomatoes

150 ml (¹/4 pint) olive oil

2 tablespoons honey

¹/2 teaspoon salt

¹/4 teaspoon ground white pepper

Preheat the oven to 140°C/275°F/Gas Mark 1.

Heat a dry frying-pan and toast the sesame seeds for 2 minutes while stirring. Keep aside on a plate. Put the tomatoes in an ovenproof dish, add the olive oil and bake for about 20 minutes. Remove from the oven and leave to cool. Then quarter the tomatoes and remove and discard the skin and seeds. Cut the tomato flesh into small cubes, about 1 cm (¹/2 inch).

Bring the honey to the boil in a saucepan and lower the heat. Add the tomatoes and season with salt and pepper. Leave to simmer for 2 minutes. Put in a serving dish and sprinkle with the sesame seeds. Leave to cool before eating.

Aubergines can be cooked and prepared in lots of different ways; however, when fried they have a tendency to soak up oil like a sponge. In order to avoid that and yet be able to fry aubergines with oil, Mrs Penina Edery has given us a useful trick: lightly beat two egg whites, adding $1/2$ teaspoon salt and 1 tablespoon white-wine vinegar and quickly soak the aubergines cubes or slices, according to recipe, before frying them. The egg white wraps the aubergine in a kind of oil-proof thin film which gives a crisp outside and moist inside. The miracle is that you find the same quantity of oil before and after the frying, in the pan and not in the aubergines. So from now on, don't hesitate to fry aubergines.

The following recipe combines four typical flavours of Morocco: aubergines, peppers, olives and pickled lemon.

four flavour salad

Traditional recipe:

SERVES 5 AS A SALAD OR STARTER

3 green peppers

3 aubergines

2 egg whites, lightly beaten

1 tablespoon white-wine vinegar

$1/2$ teaspoon salt

300 ml ($1/2$ pint) sunflower oil

$1/2$ pickled lemon

150 g ($5^1/2$ oz) green olives

2 tablespoons olive oil

juice of 1 lemon

$1/2$ teaspoon salt

1 tablespoon finely chopped fresh flat-leaved parsley, to garnish

Preheat the oven to 180°C/350°F/Gas Mark 4.

Grill the peppers on all sides, in the preheated oven, for 20 minutes, until the skin gets black.

Meanwhile, cut off the two ends of the aubergines. Wash the aubergines and dry them with kitchen paper. Cut them into 1 cm ($1/2$-inch) cubes without peeling them. Coat them in the salted egg-white-and-vinegar mixture as explained in the introduction and then fry them in the sunflower oil, until they are golden brown. Remove them from the oil, drain on kitchen paper, leave to cool and keep aside.

Remove the peppers from the oven, wrap them in a plastic bag so that they are easier to peel and leave to cool. Once cool, peel them thoroughly and remove the seeds. Slice them first into strips and cut the strips in two or three pieces if they are too long. Set aside to drain in a colander.

Remove the flesh from the pickled lemon, keep the peel, rinse it and dry it with kitchen paper. Cut it first into strips and then into 5 mm ($1/4$-inch) pieces. Keep aside.

Stone the olives and cut them into 5 mm ($1/4$-inch) pieces. Keep aside.

In a large bowl, gently mix the four ingredients. Season with the olive oil, lemon juice and salt.

Pour the salad into a serving plate and sprinkle with the chopped parsley.

hot and sweet
orange and black olive salad

With its sweet, salty and hot flavours, the hot and sweet orange and black olive salad offers an interesting mixture of contrasts. It is seasoned with *sahka*, a Moroccan home-made dried red pepper purée with a special seasoning, equivalent to what the Tunisians call *harissa*.

Sahka is used either as a side relish with fried fish or the *Mhemmer* omelette (see page 64), or as part of the seasoning in different cooked salads: steamed aubergines, carrots with cumin, swiss chards, beetroots. Home-made *sahka* is quite long to prepare, we recommend that you make a large quantity of the dried red pepper purée at once and freeze it in small containers before seasoning. Then, whenever needed, the pepper purée is left to defrost slowly and the different ingredients are added in order to obtain a *sahka* as explained in the recipe. If you don't want to go through the long process of cleaning, soaking and mincing to make the red pepper purée, you can buy it ready-made in Chinese or Middle-Eastern stores and season it with the other *sahka* ingredients as explained. *Sahka* can more effectively replace the paprika in the *chermoula* sauce (see page 80).

Traditional recipe:

SERVES 4 AS A SALAD OR STARTER

For the sahka:
500 g (1 lb 2 oz) dried sweet or hot red peppers
1 garlic clove, very finely crushed
100 ml (3^1/$_2$ fl oz) white-wine vinegar
100 ml (3^1/$_2$ fl oz) sunflower oil
2 tablespoons cold water
1^1/$_2$ teaspoons ground cumin
1 teaspoon salt

For the salad:
4 juicy and sweet oranges
100 g (3^1/$_2$ oz) salted and wrinkled black olives
1 garlic clove, crushed (optional)
^{1}/$_4$ teaspoon salt
1 teaspoon ground cumin
2 tablespoons olive oil
1 tablespoon *sahka*

In this recipe, the *sahka* can be replaced with ^{1}/$_3$ teaspoon of Cayenne pepper and a teaspoon of paprika.

To make the *sahka*, remove the stalks, white strips and seeds from the peppers and soak them in warm water for two hours. Drain them and mince them in a meat-mincer. It is recommended to protect your hands with kitchen gloves if you use hot peppers. Then add all the *sahka* ingredients to the pepper purée and mix thoroughly. *Sahka* is now ready to be used. Once seasoned, *sahka* can be kept in the fridge for one week. If you wish to keep for one more week, add the garlic at the last minute.

Peel the oranges, removing completely the pith and pips, and cut their flesh into 1 cm (^{1}/$_2$-inch) cubes. Stone the olives and cut them in half. In a bowl, put the olives and then the oranges. Add the crushed garlic clove, salt, cumin, olive oil and *sahka*. Mix all the ingredients thoroughly but very gently and serve immediately while the salad still has its beautiful individual colours and before the olives have blackened the oranges.

SOUK DES
TAILLEURS
DE PIERRE

carrot salad

with orange juice and orange-blossom water

Traditional recipe:

SERVES 4 AS A SALAD OR STARTER

500 g (1 lb 2 oz) carrots

2 juicy oranges

juice of 3 oranges

juice of 1 lemon

3 tablespoons orange-blossom water

3 tablespoons caster sugar

1/4 teaspoon salt

1/4 teaspoon ground white pepper

1 teaspoon ground cinnamon

Peel the carrots and grate into a serving bowl. Carefully peel the oranges and remove the pith and pips. Cut the flesh into cubes and add to the grated carrots.

Mix the orange juice, lemon juice, orange-blossom water, sugar, salt and pepper and pour on to the carrots and oranges. Cover with cling film and refrigerate. Sprinkle on the cinnamon before serving, chilled.

Clockwise from top left: a street in Fez; Carrot Salad with Orange Juice and Orange-Blossom Water;
Moroccan screen in Marrakech; street sign in Fez (souk of the stone-cutters)

mechouia
roasted pepper and tomato salad

Traditional recipe:

SERVES 5 AS A SALAD OR STARTER

7 large tomatoes

4 green peppers

3 tablespoons olive oil

2 garlic cloves, crushed

4 tablespoons chopped fresh coriander

1 teaspoon paprika

1 teaspoon salt

1/2 teaspoon ground white pepper

1/2 teaspoon ground cumin

Preheat the oven to 180°C/350°F/Gas Mark 4.

Roast the tomatoes and peppers in the oven, for about 20 minutes or until the pepper skins are black and blistering. Put the peppers in a plastic bag and leave till cool enough to handle. Then remove the skin and seeds. Peel the tomatoes and de-seed them.

Heat the oil in a saucepan, add the tomatoes and garlic and leave to cook to a purée, for about 15 minutes. While cooking, mash the tomatoes with a wooden spoon.

Cut the pepper flesh into small pieces and add to the tomato purée. Mix in well and then add the coriander, paprika, salt and pepper. Leave to cook for 20 minutes, stirring from time to time. Halfway through the cooking, add the cumin. Serve the *mechouia* cold.

zaalouk

Traditional recipe:

SERVES 5 AS A SALAD OR STARTER

1 kg (2¼ lb) aubergines

1 kg (2¼ lb) tomatoes

150 ml (¼ pint) olive oil

3 garlic cloves, crushed

4 tablespoons chopped fresh flat-
leaved parsley

4 tablespoons chopped fresh coriander

1 teaspoon salt

½ teaspoon ground white pepper

1 teaspoon ground cumin

Preheat the oven to 200°C/400°F/Gas Mark 6 and roast the aubergines whole for about 30 minutes or until soft. Put the tomatoes, coated in half the olive oil in another oven tray and cook them at the same time as the aubergines.

Leave until cool enough to handle, then peel the aubergines and chop the flesh. The easiest way to do this is to cut the aubergines in half lengthways and to remove the flesh with a soup spoon, avoiding the grilled skin. Peel, de-seed and mash the tomatoes coarsely with a wooden spoon.

Heat the remaining olive oil in a large pan, add the garlic and tomatoes and cook for 10 minutes. Add the chopped aubergines, parsley and coriander and season to taste with salt and pepper. Leave to cook for 20 minutes, stirring occasionally. Add the cumin, stir well and leave to cool. Serve cold.

The main ingredient in *zaalouk* is the aubergine, which is, just like broad bean, one of the most popular vegetables throughout North Africa.

Aubergine is cooked in all the different manners: steamed, fried (see Four Flavour Salad, page 58), baked, cooked and used either as a vegetable with lamb or beef or chicken, or as one of the ingredients in the couscous stock, or served cold in salads, with herbs and spices, cumin, garlic, parsley, peppers, pickled lemon. Other variants of *zaalouk* include peppers and courgettes.

The son of a shoemaker goes barefoot and the son of a weaver goes naked.

Arabic proverb

Mhemmer is a Moroccan Jewish thick omelette with potatoes. *Mhemmer* means 'reddened', due to the deep golden brown colour of the omelette soft crust. We give here the basic recipe of *mhemmer*. But there are several variants: adding peas and diced carrots for the colour and the taste, or lamb brains and breadcrumbs soaked in chicken stock (this recipe is reserved for weddings or festive meals and is known as *meguina*), or its Tunisian version known as *minina*.

Mhemmer can be eaten cold or warm. It is cut into thick slices and usually served either with a quartered lemon, or with *sahka* (see page 59), or *Merk Hzina* Salad (see opposite), or *Mechouia* (see page 62).

mhemmer
omelette cake

Traditional recipe:

SERVES 4 AS A STARTER

8 small potatoes (the size of an egg)

1¹/₂ teaspoons salt

2 litres (3¹/₂ pints) water

8 eggs

6 tablespoons chopped fresh flat-leaved parsley

¹/₂ teaspoon ground turmeric

¹/₂ teaspoon meatball spices (see page 93)

¹/₂ teaspoon baking powder

¹/₂ teaspoon ground white pepper

1 teaspoon sunflower oil

juice of 1 lemon (optional)

100 ml (3¹/₂ fl oz) sunflower oil

Peel the potatoes and cook them in the 2 litres (3¹/₂ pints) boiling water, with ¹/₂ teaspoon salt added, until soft enough to purée. Mash them coarsely with a fork while still hot. Then start adding the eggs one after the other while mixing them with a fork into the mashed potatoes. Add the parsley and continue to mix. Then add the remaining salt and all the remaining ingredients, except the sunflower oil and mix them in thoroughly.

Heat the 100 ml (3¹/₂ fl oz) sunflower oil in a small, thick-based non-stick pan and pour in the mixture. It should be in a layer of 4–5 cm (2 inches) high. Once cooked, *mhemmer* will swell. Cover and cook on very low heat for 15–20 minutes until the edges take a golden colour. Then check if *mhemmer* is cooked inside by plunging a knife in the centre and removing it. *Mhemmer* is cooked if the knife remains clean.

Preheat the grill of the oven to 180°C/350°F/Gas Mark 4 and put in the *mhemmer* uncovered for 10 to 15 minutes until the surface becomes golden brown. Alternatively, *mhemmer* can be entirely cooked in the oven.

Put a few sheets of kitchen paper on a large plate and invert the *mhemmer* on the plate to remove excess oil. Leave to cool and serve warm or cold as explained in the introduction. Leftover *mhemmer* should be covered with cling film and kept out of the fridge.

merk hzina salad

Traditional recipe:

SERVES 4 AS A SALAD OR STARTER

4 large red tomatoes, peeled and
de-seeded

1 celery heart

4 spring onions

$^1/_2$ red pepper, de-seeded

$^1/_2$ green pepper, de-seeded

$^1/_2$ pickled lemon (see page 141)

50 g (1$^3/_4$ oz) green olives

3 tablespoons chopped fresh
flat-leaved parsley

3 tablespoons chopped fresh coriander

juice of $^1/_2$ lemon

4 tablespoons sunflower oil

1 teaspoon salt

Cut the tomato flesh in pieces of 1 cm ($^1/_2$ inch). All the other vegetables should be cut into pieces about 5 mm ($^1/_4$ inch) big. Remove the flesh from the pickled lemon, keep the peel, rinse it and dry it with kitchen paper. Cut it first into strips and then into 5 mm ($^1/_4$ inch) pieces. Stone the olives and cut them into 5 mm ($^1/_4$-inch) pieces.

In a large bowl, mix gently all the ingredients (tomatoes, pickled lemon, olives, parsley, coriander, celery, spring onion, red pepper, green pepper) and then season with lemon juice, oil and the salt. Serve immediately before the salt marinates the ingredients.

soup of chick-peas,
pumpkin and aniseed

Modern recipe:

SERVES 6

200 g (7 1/2 oz) chick-peas

4 cloves

2 onions

2 soup spoons aniseeds

6 parsley sprigs

1 celery stick

1 bay leaf

500 g (1 lb 2 oz) peeled and de-seeded
pumpkin, cubed

1 soup spoon salt

1/2 teaspoon ground white pepper

1.5 litres (2 3/4 pints) milk

150 g (5 1/2 oz) butter

Soak the chick-peas in plenty of water for 24 hours before you want to make the soup. Rinse them under running water. Then put them in a pan with fresh water to cover, bring to the boil and cook for 45 minutes or until soft. Leave until cool enough to handle, then scoop them out with a slotted spoon and remove and discard their skins by pinching between your fingers. Keep aside.

Stick two cloves in each onion. Put the aniseeds in a small white muslin bag. Tie up together the parsley, celery and bay leaf in a *bouquet garni*. Put the pumpkin cubes, onions, salt and pepper in a large pan, pour in the milk and add the *bouquet garni* and the aniseeds. Bring to the boil and turn the heat down to low. Cook for 1 hour, or until the pumpkin is soft.

Remove the onion, aniseeds and *bouquet garni*. Check that the cloves are still in the onions, otherwise remove them from the stock. While still hot, blend the pumpkin in the milk until smooth. Return to a clean pan, cut the butter into pieces, add it off the heat and stir until melted. Heat the chick-peas quickly in their cooking water, drain them thoroughly and add them to the soup before serving.

Street in Chechaouen, 'The blue town'

harira

Harira is a generic name used in Morocco to designate soups made with cereals. This recipe is the one of the traditional rich and thick *harira* that Moroccan Muslims eat during *ramadan* to break the fast. *Harira* is also frequently eaten for breakfast and one can find it in the little street corner restaurants in the *medina* of Marrakech, served in a clay bowl with a deep wooden spoon. One of those *harira* places is sponsored by a rich Moroccan man who pays for the daily '*harira* production' of that restaurant, to allow the poor people to go there and have their daily bowl of *harira* free. *Harira* has been widely adopted by the Jewish communities in Morocco and Algeria and belongs henceforth to their traditional gastronomic heritage.

In the following recipe, meat and marrow-bones can be replaced with chicken stock and saffron can be replaced with $1/3$ teaspoon of ground turmeric.

The 'trick' to getting non-doughy vermicelli in the stock is to toast them gently before use in a dry frying-pan on low heat, stirring constantly until they reach a beautiful golden colour. A large quantity can be toasted at once and kept in a dry airtight jar.

How to prepare saffron Saffron, the most noble spice, is very expensive and quite subtle to use because of its intense flavouring and colouring power that gives the dishes a special taste and a wonderful golden yellow colour. Preparing the saffron first, by turning the strands into a delicate diluted powder, allows for a more effective use. Some recipes may require you to use the strands directly, but this generally doesn't give a good distribution of the flavour, taste and colour. Once prepared, saffron can be kept in the refrigerator for three or four weeks. 1 teaspoon of saffron strands will give 250 ml (8 fl oz) of prepared saffron.

Heat a dry frying-pan on a very low heat and toast the saffron strands very slowly, constantly checking and stirring with a wooden spoon for 2–3 minutes. When the saffron strands have reached a deep red colour (not too brown), put them straight away in a wooden mortar. Crush them very finely while still hot. The mortar can be replaced with a small bowl and wooden spoon. Pour the powder into a dry jar, making sure that you collect every precious grain, and fill the jar with 250 ml (8 fl oz) of warm water. Close it tightly and shake it thoroughly to allow all the saffron powder to dilute in the water. The water immediately takes a beautiful orange colour. Leave to cool and refrigerate.

Use 50 ml (2 fl oz) or 100 ml ($3^1/_2$ fl oz) of prepared saffron according to the recipe. Always shake the jar before use.

Traditional recipe:

SERVES 6

100 g (3¹/2 oz) chick-peas

100 g (3¹/2 oz) lentils

1 teaspoon bicarbonate of soda

100 ml (3¹/2 fl oz) sunflower oil

250 g (9 oz) or 3 medium-size onions, chopped

1 celery heart and 2 or 3 celery sticks, chopped

500 g (1 lb 2 oz) boneless lean lamb or beef, cubed

2 marrow-bones

1 teaspoon salt

1 teaspoon ground white pepper

2 litres (3¹/2 pints) water

3 tablespoons wheat flour

300 ml (¹/2 pint) water

1 tablespoon concentrated tomato purée plus 2 tablespoons water

1 kg (2¹/4 lb) fresh tomatoes, skinned, de-seeded and diced

100 g (3¹/2 oz) toasted vermicelli

100 g (3¹/2 oz) round-grain rice

100 ml (3¹/2 fl oz) prepared saffron

juice of 2 lemons

6 tablespoons finely chopped fresh parsley

6 tablespoons finely chopped fresh coriander

3 lemons, halved, to serve

The day before, soak the chick-peas and the lentils separately in cold water with bicarbonate of soda added (¹/2 teaspoon each). The next day, rinse the lentils thoroughly with cold water. Drain and keep aside. Boil the chick-peas for 20 minutes in their soaking water. Drain the chick-peas and leave them to cool before removing the skins by pinching them between your fingers. Rinse them thoroughly under running cold water. Drain and keep aside.

Heat the oil in a stockpot or large pan and add the onions and celery. Fry gently for 5–8 minutes until softened. Add the meat, bones, chick-peas and lentils, salt and pepper. Cover with the 2 litres (3¹/2 pints) water of water. Bring to the boil and cover the pan. Then lower the heat and leave to cook slowly for 1¹/2 hours. If necessary, skim with a slotted spoon of any froth that may rise to the surface because of the meat and marrow-bones.

Remove the marrow-bones after 1 hour and keep them aside on a plate. Check the meat after 1 hour to see if tender and remove it from the stock when cooked to prevent it from disintegrating. When cooked, remove the meat and keep aside, covered with foil to prevent from drying. Re-heat the meat in the stock before serving. The marrow-bones can be heated later on and the marrow eaten separately, sprinkled with coarse salt, on toasted country bread.

After 1¹/2 hours, mix the flour with the 300 ml (¹/2 pint) of water. Dilute the tomato purée in the 2 tablespoons of water and add both to the stockpot. Stir with a wooden spoon long enough to distribute the flour and tomato purée in the stock. Then add the tomatoes, the vermicelli, the rice, and the saffron. Stir the last ingredients with a wooden spoon, cover the pan and leave to cook for 30 minutes on medium heat.

Ten minutes before the end of the cooking, add the lemon juice and stir it well into the soup. Finally add the chopped parsley and coriander and stir well. *Harira* must be smooth but not too thick. Before serving, check and adjust the seasoning.

Harira is served hot in a bowl or soup plate with a half-lemon to add lemon juice to taste.

hot and spicy 'cigars of miga'

Many North African specialities use a dough sheet as thin as cigarette paper. Called *ouarka* in Morocco, *dioul* in Algeria and *malsouqua* in Tunisia, this pastry sheet was traditionally home-made. One can now find it easily in large supermarkets or in oriental shops. Each pack contains a number of pastry sheets separated from each other with a special sheet of paper to prevent them from sticking together. The pack is sealed to keep the pastry sheets damp and prevent them from breaking. Unopened packs keep very well in the freezer. The *ouarka* dough is made with wheat flour, unlike its Asian cousin, made with rice flour, and used to make spring rolls. The *ouarka* may be stuffed with various kinds of sweet or salty fillings and be folded, at your choice, in a triangular or rectangular shape, or rolled in the shape of cigars (as for this recipe), or in the shape of a round purse, or in *papillottes* like a candy paper. Always delicious and crisp, once stuffed, the *ouarka* becomes a *brioua* in Morocco, a *bourek* in Algeria and a *brik* in Tunisia.

Our recipe is a traditional Moroccan Jewish one which uses *miga* to fill the cigars. *Miga* is probably a word of Spanish origin meaning 'breadcrumbs' as the Judaeo-Arab spoken by the Jews in Morocco uses lots of Spanish words, sometimes corrupted. The *miga briouats* are called *pastels* by the Jews. *Miga* stuffing is also used to make small potato rissoles, called potato *pastels* or a large potato *pastela*, a sort of shepherd's pie, also called *pastela del karba* as it was traditionally cooked in the *karba*, a large enamel bowl.

You can, if you wish, freeze the cigars before you fry them. Serve them hot with drinks or as starters.

The father is unfaithful;
the mother is jealous;
the daughter at home
is perplexed.

Arabic proverb

Traditional recipe:

MAKES 96

For the filling (miga):

2 tablespoons sunflower oil

250 g (9 oz) calves' liver

250 g (9 oz) ground beef

50 g (1³/₄ oz) beef fat (optional) or

100 ml (3¹/₂ fl oz) sunflower oil

6 tablespoons chopped fresh

flat-leaved parsley

2 bay leaves

1 onion, grated

1 small potato, grated

4 garlic cloves

1 teaspoon salt

¹/₂ teaspoon ground white pepper

1 teaspoon paprika

¹/₂ teaspoon grated nutmeg

¹/₂ teaspoon ground mace

juice of 1 lemon

400 ml (14 fl oz) water

1 teaspoon ground cumin

¹/₂ teaspoon Cayenne pepper

For the cigars:

24 ouarka pastry sheets (see opposite)

1 egg white, lightly beaten

500 ml (18 fl oz) sunflower oil

Fry the calves' liver in a very little oil and then cut it in small pieces. Put it together with all the *miga* ingredients, except the cumin and the Cayenne pepper, to cook in a pan, on low heat. Stir regularly until all the water has completely evaporated. *Miga* must be very dry, once cooked.

Remove and discard the bay leaves, add the cumin and Cayenne pepper and mince the *miga* in a food processor until all the ingredients are as fine as a pâté. Correct the seasoning to taste and leave to cool.

Then form with your hands little cigars of *miga* of about 6 cm (2¹/₂ inches) long and 1 cm (¹/₂ inch) diameter, with tapering ends, until all the *miga* is used. Leave the little 'cigars' on a plate or small tray as you form them.

Cut each round *ouarka* sheet in four equal triangular parts. Spread one triangle of *ouarka* on your working surface with the round edge towards you. Put one cigar of *miga* on the sheet, close to the round edge. Fold the left and right side of the sheet so that they exceed the filling by 5 mm (¹/₄ inch) on each side. Then roll the sheet till its end. To seal the cigar, put a little beaten egg white on the angle of the *ouarka* to stick it on the roll.

Replace the cigars on the tray as you make them, with the stuck part underneath to allow it to dry without re-opening. Continue in the same manner until you have used all *miga* and *ouarka*. At this stage you can freeze the cigars if you wish to fry them later, by arranging them in a plastic storage container.

If you wish to eat them right away, heat the 500 ml (18 fl oz) of sunflower oil in a non-stick pan and fry as many cigars as fit in the pan at once, for 3 minutes on each side until they are golden. Drain them on kitchen paper and serve them hot with a drink or as starters.

briouats of saffron chicken

Briouats is the Moroccan name for small triangular or rectangular parcels filled with a variety of stuffings, ranging from *miga* (see page 71), shredded preserved tuna and hard-boiled eggs with chopped fresh flat-leaved parsley, *pastilla* filling (see page 77), soft paste cheese, shrimps, crispy vegetables (see page 207), mashed potatoes, spinach and ricotta with nutmeg (a more modern recipe), chicken (like in our recipe) to sweet almond paste with orange-blossom water (see page 135), or *mroziya* (see page 130). They freeze perfectly well before they are shallow-fried and are served, according to the recipe, either hot as a starter or appetiser, or cold as a sweet honeyed pastry. Algerians call them *boureks* and Tunisians *briks*.

Traditional recipe:

SERVES 6

For the filling:

350 g (12 oz) boneless, skinless chicken breasts

2 tablespoons olive oil

1 onion, finely chopped

1 garlic clove, crushed

50 ml (2 fl oz) prepared saffron (see page 68)

4 tablespoons chopped fresh coriander

^{1}/2 teaspoon salt

^{1}/2 teaspoon ground white pepper

2 tablespoons water

For the briouats:

8 ouarka sheets (see page 70)

300 ml (^{1}/2 pint) sunflower oil

1 lemon, sliced, to serve

Cut the chicken breasts in small fillets. In a frying-pan, heat a tablespoon of olive oil and fry the onion and garlic until golden. Remove the onion and garlic and keep aside on a small plate. Add the other tablespoon of olive oil to the pan, then the chicken fillets and fry them until browned. Then add the prepared saffron and the coriander and return the onion and garlic to the pan. Season with salt and pepper. Add the 2 tablespoons of water, stir well and leave to cook, uncovered, for 10 minutes.

Leave to cool and then turn the mixture out on to a chopping board and chop it finely with a sharp knife.

Cut each *ouarka* sheet in three strips, each 5 cm (2 inches) wide. Keep one end of the strip straight and cut the other end diagonally. Spread one strip of *ouarka* on your working table. Put a spoonful of filling close to the straight end of the strip and keep on folding in a triangular shape till the end of the paste strip. To close the *brioua*, slide the diagonal end of *ouarka* into the last slot of the *brioua* (as you would do for an unsealed envelope). Leave the *briouats* on a tray as you make them. Continue in the same manner until you have used all the filling and *ouarka*. At this stage you can freeze the *briouats* if you wish to fry them later, by arranging them in a plastic storage container.

If you wish to eat them right away, heat the 300 ml (^{1}/2 pint) of sunflower oil in a non-stick pan and fry as many *briouats* as fit in the pan at once, for 2 minutes on each side until they are golden. Drain them on kitchen paper and put four *briouats* on each serving plate, with a slice of lemon. Serve hot.

seafood rghaif

Traditional recipe:
SERVES 4

For the dough:
400 g (14 oz) wheat flour
1¹/₂ teaspoons salt
250 ml (9 fl oz) sunflower oil
20 g (³/₄ oz) fresh yeast, diluted in
100 ml (3¹/₂ fl oz) water
400 ml (14 fl oz) warm water
1 egg yolk

For the stuffing:
200 g (7¹/₂ oz) small raw prawns
200 g (7¹/₂ oz) small squid
500 ml (18 fl oz) water
1¹/₂ teaspoons salt
juice of 4 juicy lemons
6 parsley sprigs
3 tablespoons olive oil
3 onions, finely chopped
1 garlic clove, crushed
4 tablespoons finely chopped fresh flat-leaved parsley
6 tablespoons finely chopped fresh coriander
1 teaspoon paprika
¹/₄ teaspoon Cayenne pepper
1 teaspoon ground cumin

Put the flour in a large bowl in a mound with a well in the middle. Add in the salt, 200 ml (7 fl oz) of the oil and yeast, mix and pour the water slowly while kneading for about 20 minutes until you get a smooth, rubbery and rather soft dough. Oil your hands and the surface of the dough and split it in 12 equal balls. Leave to rise on an oiled plate.

Shell the prawns completely, cut them in half and de-vein them. Keep aside. Clean the squid and cut them in short, thin slices. Keep aside.

Prepare a poaching juice with water, half the salt, three-quarters of the lemon juice and the parsley sprigs and bring it to the boil. Put the heat to medium, add the squid, leave to cook for 4 minutes, then add the prawns and leave to cook for 3 more minutes. Drain the seafood and discard the parsley sprigs.

Heat the olive oil in a frying-pan, add the onions and garlic and fry until golden brown. Add the chopped parsley and coriander, paprika, Cayenne pepper and the remaining salt and continue frying for 3 minutes while stirring. Then add the remaining lemon juice and the cumin and stir well. Off the heat, mix the seafood into the onion and herb mixture. Leave to cool.

Preheat the oven to 180°C/350°F/Gas Mark 4.

To assemble the *rghaif*: on an oiled work surface, spread the dough balls with oiled fingers into a round shape, as thin as you can. Put a large tablespoonful of the filling in the centre. Fold the dough sheet several times on the four sides to cover the stuffing until you get a rough square of 8 cm (3 inches). Oil an oven tray and arrange the *rghaif* on the tray. Brush each *rghaif* with the egg yolk. Bake in the oven for 30 minutes or until golden. Serve three *rghaif* per person.

> If I am a prince and if you are a prince, who is going to drive the donkeys?
>
> Arabic proverb

Pastilla (also called *b'stella*) is a rich and savoury festive dish, traditionally served hot as a first course. It uses *ouarka* pastry sheets and a pigeon and almond sweet and spicy filling. It can be made either as a large pie, like in the photograph, to be shared between several persons or in round individual portions or even in triangles, as for *Briouats* of Saffron Chicken (see page 73) and served as an appetiser. The *pastilla briouats* can be prepared in large quantity and frozen before baking.

In our recipe, pigeon can be replaced by chicken. There are other versions of *pastilla*, with seafood and even a dessert, Milk *pastilla*, made with a thickened milk sauce (see page 128). Baking the *pastilla* in the oven instead of frying it makes it lighter.

pigeon pastilla

Traditional recipe:
SERVES 6

4 tablespoons sunflower oil
1.5 kg (3 lb 5 oz) onions, chopped
2 teaspoons grated fresh root ginger
$1/2$ teaspoon ground mace
$1/2$ teaspoon ground nutmeg
$1/4$ teaspoon ground cloves
1 teaspoon salt
1 teaspoon ground white pepper
$1^1/2$ teaspoons ground cinnamon
150 ml ($1/4$ pint) water
3 oven-ready pigeons
250 g (9 oz) blanched almonds
(see page 135)
8 eggs
50 g ($1^3/4$ oz) unsalted butter
6 tablespoons finely chopped fresh coriander
6 tablespoons finely chopped fresh flat-leaved parsley
100 ml ($3^1/2$ fl oz) prepared saffron (see page 68)
75 g ($2^3/4$ oz) granulated brown sugar
6 *ouarka* pastry sheets (see page 70)
1 egg white, lightly beaten
To garnish:
75 g ($2^3/4$ oz) icing sugar
6 mint sprigs

In a large saucepan, heat the oil and add the onions to fry gently for 5–7 minutes until softened and start colouring. Add the fresh ginger, mace, nutmeg, cloves, half the salt and pepper, 1 teaspoon of cinnamon and the water. Stir all the ingredients to mix them together. Season the pigeons inside and outside with salt and pepper to taste and add them to the preparation. Bring to the boil and cover. Then lower the heat and leave to simmer slowly for 1 hour, checking occasionally that the dish isn't drying out. If necessary, add a little water.

Toast the blanched almonds in a dry frying-pan by stirring constantly with a wooden spoon until golden. Leave them to cool out of the pan and then grind them coarsely. Keep aside.

Once cooked, remove the pigeons and leave them to cool on a plate. If the remaining cooking sauce is too thin, boil it until it is reduced to a thick sauce.

Once the pigeons are cool, remove the skin, take all the flesh from the bones and shred it coarsely with your fingers. Keep the pigeon flesh aside.

Break the eggs into a bowl and beat them thoroughly, then add them to the onions. Stir well and add the butter, coriander, parsley, saffron, sugar and remaining salt and pepper. Cook for 15 minutes on very low heat, stirring constantly until the eggs are scrambled and set, approximately during the first 8 minutes and then continue stirring occasionally for 7 more minutes. Leave to cool.

Preheat the oven to 180°C/350°F/Gas Mark 4.

Cut each round *ouarka* sheet in half. Each individual *pastilla* will use two halves. Lay out half a sheet of *ouarka* on a lightly greased non-stick individual pie tin (10 cm/4 inches in diameter). Then lay out the second half of *ouarka* on top of the first in a cross shape. Cover it with a layer of stuffing 1 cm (1½ inch) thick, scatter the shredded pigeon on top of it and sprinkle almonds all over the pigeon. Before folding the edges of *ouarka*, cut them if, once folded, they would hang over the edges of the tin. Fold the first edge of *ouarka* to cover the stuffing, brush the inside of the second edge with egg white and seal it on the first edge. Brush the inside of the third edge with egg white and seal it on the second edge. Brush the inside of the fourth edge with egg white and seal it on the third edge in order to form a small round parcel. Repeat for the five remaining individual *pastillas* with the remaining *ouarka*, filling, shredded pigeon and almonds. Brush the top of each *pastilla* lightly with oil. Bake in the preheated oven for 15 minutes until the top of each *pastilla* gets golden.

Carefully invert each *pastilla* into its tin to cook it upside-down for 15 more minutes. If not crisp and golden enough, cook for a few more minutes. Remove all the *pastillas* from the oven and put each of them, bottom-up, on a serving plate. Dust icing sugar on the surface of each *pastilla* and make a decorative pattern with the remaining ground cinnamon. The edges of the serving plates can be decorated with icing sugar and a small sprig of fresh mint.

Another nice way to serve the *pastilla* is to save the roasted wings and thighs of the pigeons, entire, by not using them in the stuffing. Heat them in the oven, covered with foil to prevent them from drying, before serving, and put one wing and one thigh on each side of the *pastilla* on the serving plate. Serve hot.

Mountain goat herd, Chechaouen

monkfish tagine with pickled lemon

Chermoula is a marinade mainly used for fried fish or fish *tagines*. It also coats lamb shoulder, or chicken before roasting. It is very tasty, hot to taste and made with typical ingredients used in North African cuisine, like coriander, cumin and ground hot red pepper. Other recipes include pickled lemon. Moroccan Jews call it *tsermela* and add lemon juice or vinegar and flat-leaved parsley to it.

Traditional recipe:

SERVES 5 AS A MAIN COURSE

For the chermoula:

2 garlic cloves, finely crushed

4 tablespoons finely chopped fresh coriander

3 tablespoons olive oil

1 teaspoon ground cumin

2 tablespoons paprika or *sahka*

1/2 teaspoon Cayenne pepper

3/4 teaspoon salt

150 ml (1/4 pint) cold water

For the fish:

1 kg (2 1/4 lb) monkfish tail, boned, cleaned and cut into 5 serving portions

4 large, ripe tomatoes

2 green peppers

For the sauce:

6 tablespoons olive oil

1 large spoonful of *chermoula*

1 teaspoon grated fresh root ginger

100 ml (3 1/2 fl oz) prepared saffron

1/2 teaspoon salt

1/2 teaspoon ground white pepper

To serve:

15 green olives, stoned

1 pickled lemon, cut into large strips

Prepare the *chermoula* first, by mixing together all the ingredients in a large bowl. Keep aside a large spoonful of *chermoula* to add to the cooking sauce. Spread the rest of the *chermoula* over the portions of fish and leave to marinate for 3 hours. To make the sauce, mix together all the ingredients.

Skin the tomatoes and cut them in quarters. Grill the peppers for a few minutes, until blackened all over and then put them in a plastic bag until cool enough to handle. Then remove the skins, discard the seeds and slice the flesh into strips. Criss-cross the pepper strips on the base of a *tagine* dish that is large enough to take the pieces in one layer. Put the pieces of fish on top of the pepper strips. Pour the sauce over the fish and arrange the tomato quarters on top. Cook, covered, on a medium heat for 30–40 minutes.

Check that the fish is cooked and check the seasoning of the sauce. If the sauce is too runny, remove the pieces of fish to a warmed dish and reduce the sauce by boiling hard, uncovered, until it has the right consistency.

Five minutes before serving, add the olives and pickled lemon strips to the sauce to heat them. Serve each portion with some olives and pickled lemon strips.

Clockwise from top left: fishing fleet in Essaouira; fish seller in Tunis central market; fish prices chalked up; Monkfish Tagine with Pickled Lemon

king prawn tagine with braised fennel

Modern recipe:

SERVES 4 AS A MAIN COURSE

16 large or 20 medium raw king prawns

200 ml (7 fl oz) olive oil

1 teaspoon salt

1 teaspoon ground white pepper

1 onion, chopped

1 garlic clove, crushed

1 kg (2¼ lb) fresh tomatoes, skinned, de-seeded and diced

¼ teaspoon sugar

1 kg (2¼ lb) fennel bulbs, sliced thickly lengthways

2 tablespoons chopped fresh coriander

2 tablespoons chopped fresh flat-leaved parsley

Remove the heads and the shells from the king prawns, leaving only the tails. Save the heads and shells. Heat one-third of the oil in a heavy-based frying-pan and fry the prawn shells and heads with a pinch of salt and pepper quickly for 2–3 minutes on high heat, while smashing the heads with a wooden spoon to get all the juices out. Sieve the oil to remove all the shells and pour it in a clean frying-pan.

Lower the heat, then add the onion and garlic to the flavoured oil and cook for 5 minutes until softened and slightly coloured. On medium heat, add the tomatoes with salt, pepper and the sugar. The sugar, without sweetening the tomato compote, removes the sourness of the tomato and gives the compote a beautiful deep red colour. Cook uncovered, stirring occasionally and checking, until the tomatoes are soft and their water has evaporated (8–10 minutes). Set the tomato compote aside.

Put the slices of fennel in the upper part of a steamer and steam them for 8 minutes. Drain them. Then put one-third of the oil in a heavy-based frying-pan, heat it and add the steamed slices of fennel. Sprinkle a little salt and pepper on the fennel and leave it to braise gently on both sides until it takes a nice golden colour.

While the fennel is braising, heat the last third of the oil in another frying-pan and fry the prawns with a little salt and pepper, for 3–4 minutes on high heat, stirring so they are evenly coloured all over.

In a heated large *tagine* plate, dress the tomato compote after having slightly heated it. Arrange the dish by alternating the prawns and the fennel slices in a star shape on the tomato compote. Sprinkle with the fresh coriander and parsley. Cover the *tagine* and serve at once.

sea bass tagine
with potatoes

It is a tradition, in North Africa, to cook fish with vegetables and serve it in a *tagine*, or to cook it directly in the *tagine*. There is almost no limit to the imagination when combining fish and vegetables is involved and this type of *tagine* deserves a whole book of their own. Fish tagines can be made with olives, carrots, chick-peas, peppers, swiss chard, broad beans, turnips, peas, fennel, or even radishes; in a more occidental manner, they can be served with almonds or capers or with couscous in the most traditional way. There are also recipes with very tasty vegetables, like cardoons or *guernina*, or baby artichokes, that are typical to North Africa and quite hard to find in Europe.

Traditional recipe:

SERVES 6 AS A MAIN COURSE

1 teaspoon salt

1 sea bass of 1.5 kg (3 lb 5 oz)

1.5 kg (3 lb 5 oz) small potatoes

1 teaspoon ground white pepper

5 large red tomatoes, sliced

6 unpeeled garlic cloves

3 green peppers, de-seeded and cut in large strips

3 dried red peppers

100 ml (3$^{1}/_{2}$ fl oz) prepared saffron (see page 68)

100 ml (3$^{1}/_{2}$ fl oz) sunflower oil

300 ml ($^{1}/_{2}$ pint) water

1 pickled lemon (see page 141)

150 g (5$^{1}/_{2}$ oz) stoned green olives

2 green chillies

juice of 1 lemon

100 ml (3$^{1}/_{2}$ fl oz) olive oil

6 tablespoons chopped fresh coriander

Preheat the oven to 180°C/350°F/Gas Mark 4.

Sprinkle the fish with some salt and leave it for 30 minutes. Then rinse it quickly under running water and drain it. Leave it whole. Make three or four gashes on the top of the fish.

Peel, wash and slice the potatoes 7 mm ($^{1}/_{4}$ inch) thick. Sprinkle salt and pepper on the potatoes and arrange them in the bottom of a large *tagine* plate or ovenproof dish.

Save a dozen tomato slices to decorate the top of the dish and arrange the rest on top of the potatoes. Add the whole garlic cloves. Save six strips of green pepper and arrange the rest on the tomatoes.

Wash the dried red peppers, soak them in hot water for 5 minutes, drain them and remove the stalks and seeds. Cut each of them in four pieces, arrange them on the rest of the vegetables and sprinkle with more salt and pepper. Add half the saffron, the sunflower oil and the water and put into the preheated oven for 30 minutes.

Remove the flesh from the pickled lemon, keep the peel, rinse it, dry it with kitchen paper and cut it into large strips.

After 30 minutes, remove the dish from the oven, add the olives and put the whole fish on top of the vegetables. Arrange tomato slices and lemon strips on top of the fish. Arrange the remaining tomato, green peppers and the 2 green chillies around the fish. Pour the lemon juice, olive oil and the remaining saffron on the fish. Put the dish back into the oven and leave to cook for 30 minutes. After 15 minutes, sprinkle the coriander on the dish and leave it to cook for the remaining 15 minutes. Remove from the oven, cover the *tagine* plate with the *tagine* cover and serve hot.

Overleaf: Street scene viewed from a barber's shop in Essaouira

whiting balls in tomato and pepper sauce

Traditional recipe:

SERVES 6 AS A MAIN COURSE

For the tomato and pepper sauce:

1 kg (2¼ lb) tomatoes, peeled,
de-seeded and diced

2 garlic cloves, peeled

½ teaspoon salt

½ teaspoon caster sugar

4 green peppers

100 ml (3½ fl oz) sunflower oil

50 ml (2 fl oz) prepared saffron
(see page 68)

1 teaspoon paprika

¼ teaspoon Cayenne pepper

For the whiting balls:

1.5 kg (3 lb 5 oz) whiting fillets

50 g (1¾ oz) brown breadcrumbs

3 tablespoons chopped fresh
flat-leaved parsley

3 tablespoons chopped fresh coriander

1 small onion, grated

1 teaspoon salt

½ teaspoon pepper

1½ teaspoons meatball spices
(see page 93)

1 egg

3 tablespoons sunflower oil

5 tablespoons water

To cook the whiting balls:

300 ml (½ pint) water

50 ml (2 fl oz) prepared saffron

First, prepare the tomato and pepper sauce. Preheat the oven to 180°C/350°F/ Gas Mark 4. On medium heat, in a saucepan put the tomatoes with the two whole garlic cloves, the salt and sugar. The sugar, without sweetening the tomato sauce, removes the sourness of the tomatoes and gives it a beautiful deep red colour. Cook uncovered for 10 minutes, stirring occasionally and checking until the tomatoes are soft and a little water is remaining. When soft, mash the garlic cloves into the tomato sauce. Switch off the heat after 10 minutes and leave the tomatoes in the pan.

While the tomatoes are cooking, grill the peppers on all sides, in a preheated oven, for 20 minutes, until the skin is blackened. Remove from the oven, wrap them in a plastic bag so that they are easier to peel and leave to cool. Once cool peel them thoroughly and remove the seeds. Slice them first into strips and cut the strips in two pieces if they are too long.

Add the strips of peppers to the tomato sauce, with the oil, saffron, paprika and Cayenne pepper and cook again slowly for 10 more minutes while stirring occasionally. Remove from the heat and leave aside in the pan.

Mince the whiting fillets in a meat-mincer. Put the fish flesh in a large bowl and add all the other ingredients for the whiting balls. Mix everything together very thoroughly, kneading with your hands.

In a clean pan, put the 300 ml (½ pint) water with the saffron and bring to the boil. Lower the heat.

Form fish balls of 3.5 cm (1¾ inches) in diameter and cook them on medium heat in the saffron water for 10 minutes. After 10 minutes, remove them from their cooking water with a slotted spoon, avoiding the froth, and put them gently in the tomato sauce. If the tomato sauce has become too thick, you can add 2 or 3 tablespoons of the fish-ball cooking juice. Coat the whiting balls gently with the sauce. Cover and keep on cooking the fish balls in the tomato sauce for 10 more minutes. Pour the whiting balls and their sauce into a covered *tagine* and serve hot.

stuffed sardines
with chermoula

Traditional recipe:

SERVES 4 AS A MAIN COURSE

For the sardines:

24 medium-size fresh sardines

$1/4$ teaspoon salt

500 ml (18 fl oz) vegetable oil

2 lemons, quartered, to serve

For the chermoula stuffing:

2 garlic cloves, finely crushed

5 tablespoons finely chopped
fresh coriander

5 tablespoons finely chopped fresh
flat-leaved parsley

3 tablespoons olive oil

1 tablespoon ground cumin

1 tablespoon paprika

$1/4$ teaspoon Cayenne pepper (optional)

$3/4$ teaspoon salt

juice of 1 lemon

For coating the fish:

4 soup spoons wheat flour

4 eggs, beaten

$1/2$ teaspoon salt

$1/2$ teaspoon ground white pepper

Sardines *mzouwej* (means 'married'). Clean the sardines, remove the head, the backbone and the tail, wash them and dry them with kitchen paper. Spread them on a tray with the skin underneath, sprinkle a very little salt on each sardine and leave in the fridge.

Prepare the *chermoula*, as explained in Monkfish *Tagine* with Pickled Lemon (see page 80), by mixing all the ingredients well in a bowl.

Remove the sardines from the fridge. Choose 12 pairs of sardines, where the size of each pair is equal and spread the filling on one sardine in each pair, avoiding the edges. Cover each stuffed sardine with the second sardine, as you would do for an sandwich.

Heat the oil for deep-frying in a pan. Put the flour on a plate. Season the eggs with the salt and pepper and beat them in a bowl. Coat a pair of stuffed sardines with flour on both sides, removing any excess flour, then dip it very gently in the beaten egg. Slide each pair of sardines into the hot oil and fry for 2 minutes on each side. Put them on kitchen paper to absorb any excess oil. Serve three pairs of sardines and 2 lemon quarters on each serving dish. Eat warm or cold.

fillet of john dory
with confit aubergines and polenta

Modern recipe:

SERVES 4 AS A MAIN COURSE

4 fillets of John Dory

salt and pepper

1 lemon, quartered, to serve

For the polenta:

500 ml (18 fl oz) milk

125 g (4$^{1}/_{2}$ oz) corn semolina

1 garlic clove, crushed

50 g (1$^{3}/_{4}$ oz) unsalted butter

50 g (1$^{3}/_{4}$ oz) parmesan cheese, grated

$^{1}/_{2}$ teaspoon salt

$^{1}/_{2}$ teaspoon ground white pepper

For the confit aubergines:

4 aubergines

$^{1}/_{2}$ teaspoon salt

$^{1}/_{2}$ teaspoon ground white pepper

1 litre (1$^{3}/_{4}$ pints) olive oil

2 thyme sprigs

2 bay leaves

3 garlic cloves

Prepare the polenta the day before. Bring the milk to the boil, sprinkle in the corn semolina and stir with a wooden spoon to get a homogeneous mix. Leave to cook for 10 minutes, while stirring. Then add the garlic, half the butter, the parmesan, salt and pepper, stir all the ingredients and leave to cook for 10 more minutes.

Brush a baking tray with the remaining butter and pour the polenta in a 1.5 cm ($^{3}/_{4}$-inch) layer. Leave it to cool. Cover it with cling film and refrigerate.

The next day, 3 or 4 hours before the meal, preheat the oven to 120°C/225°F/Gas Mark $^{1}/_{4}$ and prepare the *confit* aubergines. Cut off the two ends of the aubergines. Make an incision lengthways on each aubergine and peel them with a sharp knife, trying to keep the peel as whole as possible. Keep the peels aside, they will be used later on to wrap the aubergines. Then cut the flesh of the aubergines in stick shapes of 9 cm (3$^{1}/_{2}$ inches) long and 1 cm ($^{1}/_{2}$ inch) thick. Season them with salt, pepper and a little olive oil and grill them until soft and a bit roasted.

Meanwhile, heat the remaining olive oil gently with the thyme, bay leaves and garlic cloves, for 4 minutes. Turn the heat off and leave to infuse.

Roll the aubergine sticks in the aubergine peels, put them on a baking tray and cover them with aluminium foil. Bake in the oven for 1 hour.

Remove the aubergine strips from the wrapping peel and, while still hot, dip them into the flavoured oil. Leave to marinate for about 1$^{1}/_{2}$ hours.

While you cook the fish and the polenta, let the aubergines drain from the oil in a strainer, then put them on kitchen paper.

Cut the polenta with a pastry cutter, choosing the shape that you like, and fry the little polenta cakes, quickly on both sides with a little butter, in a non-stick frying-pan until golden.

Sprinkle the fillets of John Dory with salt and pepper and grill them for no longer than 3 minutes on each side, according to size. They should not dry but remain moist.

To serve, put the aubergine sticks on the plate, the fish on top of the aubergines and the polenta around the fish. You can decorate with lemon quarters.

stuffed chicken

The stuffed chicken is a festive Moroccan Jewish recipe, usually served for *Shabbat* or on special occasions, like weddings or *Bar Mitzvot*. Fully boning the entire raw chicken while leaving most of the flesh on the skin and without tearing it, is probably the most delicate part in this recipe. This is done by using a very sharp knife to remove the flesh from the bones. Your butcher might do it for you if you ask him very kindly. It is worth trying as the final result is a delicious stuffed chicken eaten cold as a home-made cold cut, with a salad seasoned with lemon-vinaigrette or with pickles.

To make life easier for you, you could use the same filling in chickens' neck skins. With the entire chicken or with just the neck skin, you can prepare more than one stuffed chicken in one go and freeze them before cooking (just after the wrapping), never after as it would taste watery.

The secret of the unique taste of the stuffing is the use of meatball spices, for which, like in the case of *ras-el-hanout*, almost each person has her own recipe, mixture and proportions. We give here Mrs Penina Edery's recipe. Freshly ground spices are usually prepared on Passover's eve.

> He who borrows money in order to get married, his children shall be sold for interest.
>
> Arabic proverb

Traditional recipe:

SERVES 12 AS A MAIN COURSE

For the meatball spices:

50 g (1³/4 oz) ground mace

25 g (1 oz) grated nutmeg

20 g (³/4 oz) ground cinnamon

40 g (1¹/2 oz) ground white pepper

15 g (¹/2 oz) ground Jamaican pepper

(*nouioura*)

For the stuffed chicken:

1 oven-ready chicken of 1.5 kg (3 lb 5 oz)

1 teaspoon salt

¹/2 teaspoon ground white pepper

1 chicken gizzard

4 eggs, hard-boiled

250 g (9 oz) ground chicken breasts

250 g (9 oz) minced veal

50 g (1³/4 oz) brown breadcrumbs

1¹/2 teaspoons meatball spices

2 tablespoons chopped fresh flat-leaved

parsley

4 tablespoons sunflower oil

4 tablespoons water

For the cooking sauce:

300 ml (¹/2 pint) home-made chicken stock

(see method)

100 ml (3¹/2 fl oz) sunflower oil

juice of 1 lemon

100 ml (3¹/2 fl oz) prepared saffron

(see page 68)

¹/2 teaspoon salt

¹/2 teaspoon ground white pepper

3 garlic cloves

The given quantity of meatball spices will allow you a full year of cooking as you never use more than 1 or 2 teaspoons in each recipe requiring those spices. Freshly ground spices should always be used. To prepare the meatball spices, add all the spices together in a bowl and mix them thoroughly. Put them in a clean dry jar with an airtight lid to keep the aroma fresh.

Rinse the chicken, and bone it gently, as explained in the introduction. Spread out the chicken, skin-side underneath and sprinkle it with salt and pepper on both sides. Keep aside on a plate. Boil the carcass, bones and the gizzard with a little salt and pepper in 300 ml (¹/2 pint) water to make a quick, concentrated chicken stock.

Hard-boil four eggs, shell them, keep the yolks whole and shred two of the hard-boiled egg whites (the others are not used) and keep aside. Chop the gizzard in small pieces and keep aside.

In a large bowl, put the ground chicken and veal and add all the ingredients and spices, except the hard-boiled eggs. Mix the stuffing thoroughly, kneading with your hands, then add the shredded egg whites and the chopped gizzard and continue to mix gently so as not to disintegrate the egg whites. The filling should be soft.

Top the chicken with the filling in order to cover the whole surface. Put the four hard-boiled egg yolks on the filling at equal distance from each other. Roll the chicken in order to obtain an even round roll and to keep all the filling inside. Sew up the roll and wrap it in a clean light cloth in order to give it a perfect thick, round, sausage shape. Tie up the two ends of the cloth.

Put all the ingredients of the cooking sauce together in a large, deep saucepan and bring to the boil; then lower the heat and add the stuffed chicken. Leave to cook, covered, on medium heat for 15 minutes on one side and 15 minutes on the other side. After 30 minutes, take the wrapping off, put the chicken back into the saucepan and leave it to roast on all sides until the remaining sauce has totally evaporated and the outside of the chicken is evenly golden.

Leave to cool completely before slicing in 1.5 cm (⁵/8 inch) thick slices and serve.

mechoui

Mechoui is normally the entire lamb or mutton roasted in a deep mud oven dug in the ground. It is still prepared that way for certain holy days or family celebrations. *Aid el Adha*, one of the holiest Muslim days, celebrates an incident described in the Koran, when the angel Gabriel prevented Ibrahim from sacrificing his son, Ismail. It is the habit in Muslim families, on the Aid day, to sacrifice a sheep in commemoration. The different parts of the mutton are prepared in different manners: roasted, cooked in the couscous stock, or grilled.

The Moroccan Jews used to roast several entire lambs during the famous *hilloula*, which are whole weeks of pilgrimage that celebrate the anniversary of the death of a Saint or a Rabbi. The Muslim equivalent to the *hilloula* is the *moussem*. The most famous *moussem* gathering in Morocco is the *moussem of the fiancées* in Imilchil, a village in the Atlas mountains, a sort of huge 'blind-date party' where the families bring their daughters, superbly dressed up, made up and tattooed, with the hope of getting them engaged.

In France, where the North African community is important, *mechoui*, just like couscous, has almost become a national dish. Both were introduced to France by the *pieds noirs*, literally meaning *black feet*, or Europeans born in North Africa. For family or friends' gatherings it is not rare to be invited to a '*mechoui* party', a sort of barbecue-garden party where the *mechoui* is the centrepiece. The whole lamb is then put on a spit and roasted in a pit over a slow-burning charcoal fire. *Mechoui* can be eaten in certain little street-corner restaurants, in the *medina* of Marrakech for instance. It is served with salt and ground cumin mixed together to season. The *chouaye* is typically the name of the grill-expert, and, by extension, the name of those little mixed-grill restaurants where one can find *mechoui*, *brochettes*, *kefta*. In our recipe, we recommend shoulder of lamb, but the whole leg of lamb can also be used, though it takes longer to cook than shoulder of lamb.

Accustom your stomach to two loaves, but do not accustom your body to two garments.

Arabic proverb

mechoui with herbs

Traditional recipe:

SERVES 4 AS A MAIN COURSE

5 tablespoons chopped fresh coriander

5 tablespoons chopped fresh
flat-leaved parsley

200 g (7^1/2 oz) butter

2 garlic cloves, finely crushed

1 teaspoon dried thyme leaves

1 teaspoon ground cumin

1 teaspoon paprika

1 teaspoon salt

1 teaspoon ground white pepper

4 *mechoui* of 350 g (12 oz) on the bone,
cut from the shoulder of lamb

50 ml (2 fl oz) oil

100 ml (3^1/2 fl oz) plus 2 tablespoons
water

1 teaspoon cornflour or potato flour

To serve:

4 thyme sprigs

1 teaspoon salt

1 teaspoon ground cumin

^{1}/4 teaspoon ground pepper

Preheat the oven to 180°C/350°F/Gas Mark 4. Put aside 1 teaspoon of coriander and 1 teaspoon of parsley. Mix the butter with the garlic, remaining coriander and parsley, thyme, cumin and paprika until you get a homogenous paste. Sprinkle the salt and pepper on the lamb *mechoui*, all over, and coat them with the butter mixture.

Put the lamb *mechoui* on a roasting dish brushed with oil. Add the 100 ml (3^1/2 fl oz) of water to the dish. Cook for 35 minutes while basting regularly and turning the meat to roast it on all sides. The meat should be evenly golden brown. Lower the heat to 150°C/300°F/Gas Mark 3. Cover the dish with foil and leave to cook for 45 minutes. When cooked, the meat should almost fall off the bone.

Remove the meat from the oven and keep it aside, covered with foil. Remove excess fat from the meat juices and pour the juices into a small pan, adding the 2 tablespoons of water. Put on high heat, add the cornflour or potato flour and leave to cook uncovered for 3 minutes, while stirring. Put the meat on a *tagine* plate, pour the sauce on the meat, sprinkle with the reserved teaspoon of coriander and parsley and decorate with a small bouquet of fresh thyme sprigs. Cover the *tagine* and serve very hot.

In a very small bowl, mix together the salt, cumin and pepper and serve it together with the meat for the guests to add to taste on their meat.

Accompany with couscous (see page 114), or Potato Gratin with Fresh Coriander (see page 100).

roasted quails with semolina and almonds

The filling of semolina and almonds is used in different recipes, to stuff poultry, for example, quails, pigeons, chickens, turkey, or meat, such as lamb or veal.

Traditional recipe:

SERVES 4 AS A MAIN COURSE

1 teaspoon salt

1/2 teaspoon ground white pepper

8 small, oven-ready quails

For the stuffing:

300 g (10 1/2 oz) couscous

300 g (10 1/2 oz) blanched almonds (see page 135)

75 g (2 3/4 oz) caster sugar

50 g (1 3/4 oz) butter, melted

50 ml (2 fl oz) orange-blossom water

1 teaspoon ground cinnamon

1/2 teaspoon salt

For the sauce:

100 ml (3 1/2 fl oz) sunflower oil

5 onions, finely chopped

6 tablespoons chopped fresh coriander, finely chopped

1 teaspoon ground ginger

1 teaspoon ground cinnamon

1/2 nutmeg, finely grated

1/4 teaspoon salt

1/4 teaspoon ground white pepper

200 ml (7 fl oz) water

Preheat the oven to 180°C/350°F/Gas Mark 4.

Sprinkle salt and pepper inside and outside the quails. Keep aside.

To make the stuffing: steam the couscous according to the instructions on page 115. Allow to cool. Meanwhile, toast the almonds in a dry pan for a few minutes, until lightly browned. Allow to cool and mince them in a food processor. Mix them thoroughly with the couscous and all the other stuffing ingredients. Stuff each raw quail with an equal quantity of the filling.

To make the sauce: heat the oil in a large pan. Add the onions, coriander, ginger, cinnamon, nutmeg, salt and pepper. Fry for 2 minutes until the onions are translucent. Add the water. Bring to the boil, lower the heat and leave to cook, uncovered, for 5 minutes. Check the seasoning. Arrange the quails in an oven tray, in such a manner that they lay on one side and pour the sauce over them. Put in the oven and bake for 20 minutes on each side. Check occasionally and add a little water if necessary.

Set two quails and some juice on each serving dish and serve hot.

fennel and courgette compote
with aniseed

Modern recipe:

SERVES 4 AS A SIDE DISH

6 fennel bulbs

4 unpeeled courgettes

3 tablespoons olive oil

1 tablespoon aniseeds

20 g (3/4 oz) unsalted butter

1/2 teaspoon salt

1/2 teaspoon ground white pepper

Clean the fennel bulbs, removing all the hard parts, and chop finely. Cut the courgettes into 1 cm (1/2-inch) cubes. Heat 2 teaspoons of olive oil in a large pan, add the chopped fennel, reduce the heat and stir. When translucent, cover the pan and leave to cook on low heat for 35 minutes. Stir occasionally.

Meanwhile, heat another spoonful of oil in another pan and fry the courgettes while stirring, on medium heat, for 5 minutes, without browning. Ten minutes before the end of the fennel's cooking time, add the aniseed and the courgettes. Stir gently but thoroughly and uncover the pan for the rest of the cooking time, to allow for complete evaporation. Off the heat, add the butter, cut into small pieces, and the salt and pepper. Stir and serve hot.

Clockwise from top left: bowls at Momo; Moroccan screen; vegetable seller at Tunis market; Fennel and Courgette Compote with Aniseed

potato gratin with fresh coriander

Traditional recipe:

SERVES 5 AS A SIDE DISH

1.25 kg (2³/4 lb) potatoes

125 g (4¹/2 oz) butter

6 tablespoons chopped fresh coriander

leaves of 3 fresh thyme sprigs, chopped

1 teaspoon salt

¹/2 teaspoon pepper

Preheat the oven to 180°C/350°F/Gas Mark 4.

Peel the potatoes, wash them and dry them with kitchen paper before slicing them finely in a large bowl. Melt the butter in a heavy-based saucepan. Add the melted butter and herbs to the potatoes. Season with salt and pepper and mix thoroughly. Spread the potato mixture in a gratin dish and spread them out evenly. Cover with foil and bake for 30 minutes. Check that the potatoes are cooked. Serve hot.

spelt with fresh vegetables

Traditional recipe:

SERVES 4 AS A SIDE DISH

500 g (1 lb 2 oz) spelt

2 carrots

1 fennel bulb

1 celery stick

50 g (1³/4 oz) peas

1/2 teaspoon ground turmeric

1 teaspoon salt

1/2 teaspoon ground white pepper

750 ml (1 pint 7 fl oz) cold water

2 tablespoons olive oil

500 ml (18 fl oz) chicken stock

1 courgette

1 tablespoon chopped fresh coriander, to garnish

The day before, soak the spelt in cold water. The next day peel and dice the vegetables. In a deep pan, put the spelt together with the vegetables, except the courgette, add the spices and stir to mix everything together. Cover with cold water and bring to the boil. Lower the heat, cover the pan and let simmer for 1 hour until the water has been absorbed. If necessary, add more water if it has all been absorbed before 1 hour.

Then add the olive oil, the chicken stock and the diced courgette, cover and cook for 30 more minutes. After 15 minutes, uncover to allow evaporation.

For vegetarians, replace the chicken stock with vegetable stock. Pour in a serving dish, sprinkle with the coriander and serve hot.

Overleaf: Marrakech central market

lamb tagine
with dried fruits
·

Traditional recipe:

SERVES 6 AS A MAIN COURSE

1.6 kg (3 lb 10 oz) boneless shoulder of
lamb, cut in 100 g (3 1/2 oz) pieces

50 ml (2 fl oz) prepared saffron
(see page 68)

400 g (14 oz) onions, chopped

3 garlic cloves, crushed

2 litres (3 1/2 pints) vegetable oil

50 g (1 3/4 oz) butter

150 ml (1/4 pint) water

120 g (4 oz) flaked almonds, fried,
to garnish

For the spice mixture:

1 teaspoon ground cinnamon

1/2 teaspoon ground turmeric

1 teaspoon salt

1/2 teaspoon ground white pepper

For the dried fruits:

150 g (5 1/2 oz) dried apricots

150 g (5 1/2 oz) prunes

150 g (5 1/2 oz) dried figs

4 cinnamon sticks

Put the pieces of lamb in a large *tagine* dish. Mix together the ingredients for the spice mixture. Scatter on the spice mixture and roll the pieces of meat in the mixture. Add the prepared saffron. Put over a medium heat and add the onions, garlic, oil, butter and a 100 ml (3 1/2 fl oz) of the water. Cover and leave to cook for 1 hour.

After 30 minutes, mix the dried fruits and the cinnamon sticks in a bowl, cover with a ladleful of the meat sauce and leave to swell for 30 minutes.

Add the fruit mixture with the cinnamon sticks and the juice to the meat *tagine*, cover and leave to cook for 10 more minutes.

Before serving, remove the cinnamon sticks, arrange the meat in the centre of the *tagine* and surround it with the dried fruits, alternating the three colours, and sprinkle with the fried flaked almonds.

lamb tagine
with fresh artichokes
and peas

Traditional recipe:

SERVES 6 AS A MAIN DISH

6 large globe artichokes (or 6 frozen
artichoke hearts)

500 g (1 lb 2 oz) fresh peas in pods

1.5 kg (3 lb 5 oz) boneless lamb, cubed

1 teaspoon ground ginger

100 ml (3½ fl oz) prepared saffron
(see page 68)

2 garlic cloves, crushed

100 ml (3½ fl oz) sunflower oil

juice of 1 lemon

1 pickled lemon (see page 141)

12 olives

Remove the outer leaves of the artichokes and scoop out the 'choke', leaving the hearts. As you prepare them, drop the hearts into a bowl of water with some lemon or vinegar, to prevent them from discolouring.

Shell the peas and set them aside.

Put the meat in a large *tagine* dish, with the ginger, saffron, garlic and oil. Pour on water to cover, put on the *tagine* cover and leave to simmer on medium to low heat for 1 hour. Stir several times during cooking and add a little extra water as necessary, to prevent it from drying out.

When the meat is cooked, remove it from the *tagine* and set it aside, covered with foil to prevent it from drying.

Rinse the peas in fresh water. Put half the meat juice in a pan and leave the rest in the *tagine*. Add the peas in the pan, add enough water to cover and cook, covered for 30 minutes, on medium heat. At the same time, add the artichoke hearts to the *tagine* with the lemon juice and enough water and leave to cook, covered for 30 minutes, on medium heat.

After 20 minutes, uncover the pan and the *tagine*, raise the heat till the end of the cooking. Remove the flesh from the pickled lemon, keep the peel, rinse it and dry it with kitchen paper. Cut it into large strips. Then add the meat on top of the artichokes, pour the peas and their sauce on the meat, add the pickled lemon strips and the olives. Cover the *tagine*, bring to the boil and leave to simmer for 2 minutes. Serve immediately, very hot.

chicken tagine
with honeyed pears and cinnamon

Traditional recipe:

SERVES 4 AS A MAIN COURSE

50 ml (2 fl oz) sunflower oil

2 onions, chopped

1.25 kg (2 lb 12 oz) chicken pieces

2 cinnamon sticks

100 ml (3^1/$_2$ fl oz) prepared saffron
(see page 68)

1 teaspoon salt

^{1}/$_2$ teaspoon ground white pepper

1 bunch fresh coriander, tied with string

1 teaspoon ground ginger

250 ml (9 fl oz) water

5 pears

50 g (1^3/$_4$ oz) unsalted butter

4 tablespoons honey

50 ml (2 fl oz) orange-blossom water

2 tablespoons sesame seeds, to garnish

Heat the oil in a *tagine* plate on a low heat and put in the onions to fry gently until golden. Add the chicken, cinnamon sticks, saffron, salt, pepper, coriander and ginger. Pour in the water, stir and leave to cook, covered, for about 45 minutes.

While the chicken cooks, peel, core and quarter the pears. On low heat, melt the butter in a pan, add the honey and the pears and cook the pears, turning them gently on each side, until they are caramelised.

Ten minutes before the end of cooking, add the pears and the orange-blossom water to the *tagine* plate. Toast the sesame seeds in a dry pan until golden.

Just before serving, remove the bunch of coriander and scatter the dish with the sesame seeds. Serve hot.

chicken tagine
with olives and pickled lemon

Traditional recipe:

SERVES 5 AS A MAIN COURSE

1.5 kg (3 lb 5 oz) oven-ready chicken

1 teaspoon salt

1 teaspoon ground white pepper

125 g (4^1/$_2$ oz) purple or green cracked olives, stoned

1^1/$_2$ pickled lemons (see page 141)

50 g (1^3/$_4$ oz) butter

2 tablespoons olive oil

1 onion, finely chopped

3 garlic cloves

1 teaspoon ground ginger

100 ml (3^1/$_2$ fl oz) prepared saffron (see page 68)

500 ml (18 fl oz) water

3 tablespoons chopped fresh coriander

3 tablespoons chopped fresh flat-leaved parsley

Sprinkle the chicken with half the salt and pepper inside and outside and keep aside.

Blanch the olives three times by plunging them into boiling water. Leave to boil for 30 seconds, rinse under running water and repeat these two operations twice more. Change the boiling water each time. Drain the olives and keep them aside in a colander.

Remove and discard the flesh and pips from the pickled lemons. Rinse the peel and dry with kitchen paper, then cut in large slices. Keep aside in a small dish.

Heat the butter and oil in a heavy saucepan, add the onion and fry gently, stirring frequently until softened and translucent. Add the garlic, ginger, saffron, the remaining salt and pepper and water and stir well to mix the spices in thoroughly. Add the chicken and turn it over to coat it with the sauce. Bring to the boil. Lower the heat, cover the pan and leave to cook slowly for 1 hour, turning the chicken over several times so that all sides soak up the sauce. If necessary, add a little hot water during the cooking.

Add the olives, pickled lemon, coriander and parsley, stir, cover and cook for 15 more minutes. Check the seasoning. Once the chicken is cooked, if the sauce is too runny, remove the chicken and keep it aside, covered with foil to keep it warm. Raise the heat and boil the sauce for 5 minutes to reduce it. Put the chicken in a warmed *tagine* plate. Arrange the pickled lemon strips and olives on top. Stir the sauce and quickly pour it over the chicken. Cover the *tagine* dish and serve straight away, very hot.

chicken tagine
with chick-peas, red peppers and garlic

Traditional recipe:

SERVES 5 AS A MAIN COURSE

300 g (10^1/$_2$ oz) chick-peas

^{1}/$_2$ teaspoon bicarbonate of soda

1.5 kg (3 lb 5 oz) oven-ready chicken

2 large fresh red peppers

4 dried sweet red peppers

100 ml (3^1/$_2$ fl oz) sunflower oil

8 unpeeled garlic cloves

^{1}/$_2$ teaspoon ground turmeric

^{1}/$_4$ teaspoon Cayenne pepper

1 teaspoon salt

^{1}/$_2$ teaspoon ground white pepper

250 ml (9 fl oz) water

The day before, soak the chick-peas in cold water with bicarbonate of soda added. The next day, boil the chick-peas for 45 minutes in their soaking water. Drain the chick-peas and leave them to cool before removing the skin by pinching them between your fingers. Rinse them thoroughly under running cold water. Drain and keep aside.

Rinse the chicken and cut it into eight pieces. Cut the fresh red peppers in quarters, remove the stalks and seeds and rinse the pepper. Remove the stalks, white strips and seeds from the dried red peppers and soak them in warm water for 30 minutes. Cut each pepper into four pieces.

Heat the oil in a large *tagine* plate or a flameproof casserole dish, add the garlic, turmeric, Cayenne pepper, salt and pepper and stir. Then add the pieces of chicken, and fry on medium heat, stirring, for about 15 minutes until the pieces are an even light brown. Remove the chicken. Add the dried red peppers, then the chick-peas, then the fresh red peppers and the water and put the pieces of chicken back into the *tagine*. Cover, bring to the boil, lower the heat and leave to cook for 45 minutes. Uncover the dish and leave to simmer for 10 minutes until the sauce becomes thick and creamy. Serve very hot, covered with the *tagine* cover.

duck tagine
with apples

Traditional recipe:

SERVES 4 AS A MAIN COURSE

100 ml (3¹/₂ fl oz) oil

3 onions, chopped

¹/₂ teaspoon ground turmeric

1 teaspoon salt

¹/₂ teaspoon ground white pepper

1 teaspoon caster sugar

4 duck legs

1 teaspoon ground coriander

1 teaspoon ground ginger

salt and pepper

To serve:

150 g (5¹/₂ oz) blanched almonds
(see page 135)

25 g (1 oz) sesame seeds

4 Granny Smith apples

100 ml (3¹/₂ fl oz) orange-blossom
water

In a frying-pan, heat the oil, lower the heat and add the onions, turmeric, salt, pepper and a teaspoon of sugar. Stir and let the mixture sizzle on very low heat for 20 minutes, while stirring occasionally. Put the mixture on a plate and keep aside.

Remove the excess fat from the duck legs and sprinkle with salt and pepper. Heat a dry, medium-size non-stick saucepan, put the duck legs in the saucepan and roast them on all sides for 5 minutes. Add the coriander and ginger, cover with water, bring to the boil, lower the heat and leave to cook for 45–60 minutes according to size. Check after 45 minutes.

Toast the almonds in a pre-heated dry pan while stirring, until golden and keep aside. Toast the sesame seeds in the same pan while stirring, until golden. Keep aside.

Remove the duck legs from the cooking stock and remove all the fat from the duck stock.

Put the onions first in a layer at the bottom of the *tagine* plate. Add the duck legs and a quarter of the duck stock. Cover the *tagine*, bring to the boil, lower the heat and leave to cook for 10 minutes.

Peel and core the apples and slice them thinly horizontally. Arrange the apple slices around the duck, cover and keep on cooking for 5 minutes. Before serving, add the orange-blossom water, then add the toasted almonds and sprinkle with the sesame seeds. Cover the *tagine* and serve hot.

confit of duck tagine
with pears, figs and glazed carrots

Modern recipe:

SERVES 4 AS A MAIN COURSE

4 pieces *confit* of duck

75 g (3¹/₂ oz) unsalted butter

50 g (1³/₄ oz) sugar

3 pears, peeled, cored and cut into quarters

ground cinnamon

15 large fresh figs

4 onions, finely chopped

100 ml (3¹/₂ fl oz) duck or chicken stock

For the glazed carrots:

3 large carrots

25 g (1 oz) unsalted butter

50 g (1³/₄ oz) brown sugar

¹/₄ teaspoon salt

Put the pieces of duck in a covered pan on low heat, for 10 minutes, to melt the fat round them and then drain them thoroughly to remove excess fat. Reserve the fat.

Heat 50 g (1³/₄ oz) of the butter in a pan, add the sugar and start a caramel on low heat. Once brown, coat the quarters of pears with the caramel and sprinkle cinnamon all over them.

Wash the figs and remove the stalks, without peeling them. Cut four figs in quarters and put them aside. Dice the rest of the figs.

Put the remaining butter (25 g/1 oz) in a large pan together with the onions and cook, covered, for 10 minutes, stirring occasionally. Then add the diced figs and stir with the onions. Cover with the duck stock and leave to cook uncovered, stirring occasionally, until reduced to a soft compote of an even consistency but not dry.

Slice the carrots diagonally. Put them in a small pan, add water to cover and the butter, sugar and salt. Leave the carrots to cook uncovered on a low heat until the water has evaporated completely.

Heat 3 tablespoons of the duck fat in a frying-pan on a very low heat and put in the fig quarters on one side. Add a pinch of sugar and cinnamon on the top side of the fig quarter and fry for 1 minute. Turn the fig quarters to the other side, sprinkle with another pinch of sugar and cinnamon and fry for 1 minute.

Serve in individual warm *tagine* plates, first dividing the fig and onion compote between the *tagines*, then putting one piece of duck, completely drained from its fat, on top of the compote. Around the duck, arrange the glazed carrots and put three of the caramelised pear quarters in a dome shape. Finally, add four fig quarters to each *tagine*. Sprinkle the whole dish with a little more cinnamon. Cover each *tagine* and heat it for 2 minutes. Serve very hot.

how to prepare couscous

Couscous is the name of a grain made from a mixture of wheat semolina, wheat flour and water. Couscous used to be prepared at home in almost a scientific dosage of thin wheat semolina, flour and water, requiring above all a unique dexterity. Today, couscous is sold, ready-made, in fine-, medium- or coarse-grain versions. The finest version is used in Couscous *Seffa* (see page 127), or in couscous *mesfouf*, both of which are fairly dry varieties of couscous. The medium-grain version is normally used for all other couscous served with a stock. And the coarsest version, in which each couscous grain can be 3–4 mm/about 1/8 inch in diameter, is used for *berkouks*, a couscous with milk and butter, traditionally served either with salt or with sugar, in Morocco, on the Jewish *Pourim* holiday.

Couscous, a complete and convivial dish, has become the national dish of North Africa. Its grain is the basis of dozens of different recipes, sweet or spicy, including either vegetables, and/or meat, poultry, offal (mainly in Algeria, for instance in the famous Algerian Jewish *couscous barbouche with osbane* – a thick offal sausage) and fish (particularly in Tunisia where the Jews have elected fish couscous as the traditional Friday night *Shabbat* meal). Couscous grain, with special ingredients is also used as a stuffing. A couscous dish usually has four main ingredients: steamed grain, different vegetables, meat and stock, which can be meat and/or vegetable stock or milky stock or it can be served with buttermilk. Couscous may be accompanied by little side dishes: chick-peas, raisins and *harissa*.

Tabbouleh, a traditional Lebanese recipe, is made with *bourgoul*, a coarsely crushed wheat. In this book we have created a free-modern version of *tabbouleh* made with steamed couscous (see Sea Bass Fillet served on a Warm Tabbouleh with Citrus Fruit Juice, page 166). In our chapter on spices, you will find the 'secret spices' of couscous, usually *ras-el-hanout*.

A good couscous is one in which the steaming of the grain is perfect, meaning light, fluffy, with all the grains perfectly detached and not pasty.

The following method for steaming the couscous is the basic method for cooking any kind of couscous grain and applies to all the couscous recipes given in this book. Typically, couscous is steamed three times but it can be steamed up to seven times.

Couscous can be cooked in the steam emanating from any kind of stock, according to the recipe. First, choose your couscous grade: fine, medium or coarse, and kind of cereal: wheat semolina, barley (called *belboula* and which is more like barley grits, that is coarsely crushed barley rather than a semolina), *frik* (the Algerian crushed green wheat), or even corn semolina, according to your recipe. Once steamed, the couscous semolina will at least double its volume, so 500 g/1 lb 2 oz will serve eight people quite generously.

Traditional recipe:

SERVES 8

500 g (1 lb 2 oz) couscous (grade according to recipe)

500 ml (18 fl oz) water (for step 1)

1 teaspoon salt

300 ml (½ pint) water (to divide between steps 3, 5 and 7)

80 g (3 oz) unsalted butter, cut into small pieces

If making savoury couscous:

½ teaspoon salt

½ teaspoon pepper

½ teaspoon ground turmeric

1. Pour the dry couscous into a large dish or bowl, the *gsaa* (see page 219). Pour on 500 ml (18 fl oz) of cold, salted water, stir and leave to soak for about 1 hour, stirring from time to time. This will re-hydrate the grains.

2. One hour and 15 minutes before you want to serve the couscous, put it into the upper part of the special couscous steamer, the *couscoussier* (see page 219) without tamping down. Fit the upper part over the bubbling stock in the lower half and cook for 15 minutes from when steam begins to come up through the couscous. Check that the seal between the upper and lower parts of the *couscoussier* is perfectly hermetic, to allow the steam to go through the couscous and not to escape from the edges. If not, seal the two parts of the *couscoussier* with a band of fabric soaked in a mixture of flour and water.

3. Tip the couscous on to another dish, open it with a wooden spoon to spread the grains and allow to cool enough to handle, then sprinkle with 100 ml (3½ fl oz) water and mix the couscous by rubbing the grains with your hands. Leave to rest for about 15 minutes.

4. Replace the couscous in the steamer over the bubbling stock and cook for about 15 minutes.

5. Then repeat step 3.

6. Steam a third time for 10 minutes.

7. Then repeat step 3 and, when spreading the grains, and, only in non-sweet recipes, add salt, pepper, and a little ground turmeric to give a nice golden colour to the grain. Cut the butter in small pieces and add them to the couscous. Mix with a fork, fluffing the grains to coat them in the butter. This will prevent them from sticking together and will keep them light and fluffy. The couscous is ready to be served, together with the other ingredients.

couscous t'faya

Traditional recipe:

SERVES 4–5 AS A MAIN COURSE

For the stock:

1 kg (2¹/₄ lb) boneless lamb, cubed

1 onion, chopped

6 coriander sprigs

100 ml (3¹/₂ fl oz) prepared saffron
(see page 68)

1 teaspoon salt

¹/₂ teaspoon ground white pepper

50 ml (2 fl oz) olive oil

For the couscous:

600 g (1 lb 5 oz) medium-grade couscous

500 ml (18 fl oz) water

1 teaspoon salt

300 ml (¹/₂ pint) water

80 g (3 oz) unsalted butter, cut into pieces

For the t'faya:

150 g (5¹/₂ oz) seedless raisins

50 g (1³/₄ oz) unsalted butter

5 onions, thinly sliced

1¹/₂ teaspoons ground cinnamon

4 tablespoons brown sugar

1 tablespoon honey

1 teaspoon ground ginger

¹/₂ teaspoon salt

¹/₂ teaspoon ground white pepper

150 ml (¹/₄ pint) water

50 ml (2 fl oz) prepared saffron
(see page 68)

In the lower part (stock-pot) of a *couscoussier*, put the meat, onion, coriander sprigs, saffron, salt and pepper and olive oil and pour in enough water to fill half the stock-pot. Bring to the boil, lower the heat and fit the upper part (steamer) in order to steam the couscous as explained on page 115. Leave the meat to cook in the stock for an hour, while steaming the couscous.

Check that the meat is cooked and, if necessary, remove it to prevent it from disintegrating if the couscous steaming is not finished. In that case, don't forget to re-heat the meat in the stock before serving.

Meanwhile, prepare the *t'faya*: soak the raisins in warm water to cover and leave to swell for 15 minutes. Drain well and keep aside.

Heat the butter and fry the onions on low heat until soft and translucent. Add the cinnamon, sugar, honey, ginger, salt, pepper, water and cook on very low heat, uncovered, for 1 hour until the onions have caramelised. Stir occasionally. After 30 minutes, add the raisins and 15 minutes later, add the saffron. Put the heat to medium and keep cooking for 15 more minutes to allow for any residual evaporation, while stirring from time to time.

Put the couscous on a serving dish in a mound with a well in the middle. Put the meat in the centre, top with the *t'faya* and serve at once. The meat cooking juice can be strained and served together with the couscous, in a tureen. Serve hot.

couscous
with brochettes of lamb and chicken

Traditional recipe:

SERVES 5 AS A MAIN COURSE

For the marinade:

250 ml (9 fl oz) olive oil

juice of 3 lemons

3 onions, finely chopped

6 tablespoons finely chopped fresh flat-leaved parsley

6 tablespoons finely chopped fresh coriander

3 teaspoons ground cumin

2 teaspoons paprika

1 teaspoon salt

1 teaspoon ground white pepper

For the couscous:

1 kg (2 1/4 lb) medium-grade couscous

800 ml (1 pint 7 fl oz) water

1 teaspoon salt

80 g (3 oz) unsalted butter, cut into pieces

For the brochettes:

600 g (1 lb 5 oz) skinless chicken breasts, cut into 2 cm (3/4-inch) cubes

600 g (1 lb 5 oz) boneless lamb, cut into 2 cm (3/4-inch) cubes

Mix all the marinade ingredients together and divide between two large bowls. Add the cubes of chicken to one bowl and the cubes of lamb to the other bowl. Mix well and leave to marinate for 4 hours.

Prepare the couscous as explained on page 115.

Thread four cubes of meat onto 12 cm (5-inch) long wooden skewers. Do the same with the chicken. Preheat the grill or light the barbecue. When very hot, cook the brochettes for about 5–8 minutes, turning one or twice and brushing them with the remaining marinade occasionally. Make sure that the meat and chicken are cooked. Serve hot together with the couscous.

couscous
with chicken and pumpkin

Traditional recipe:

SERVES 6 AS A MAIN COURSE

For the stock:

1¹/₂ teaspoons cumin seeds

2 cloves

1 large onion, halved

1.5 kg (3 lb 5 oz) oven-ready chicken

1 teaspoon salt

¹/₂ teaspoon ground white pepper

250 g (9 oz) carrots, peeled and cut
into 3 cm (1¹/₂-inch) pieces

8 coriander sprigs, tied with string

3 litres (5¹/₄ pints) full-cream milk

1.5 kg (3 lb 5 oz) pumpkin, peeled,
de-seeded and cut into large cubes

250 g (9 oz) courgettes, halved
lengthways and cut into 3 cm
(1¹/₂-inch) pieces

100 ml (3¹/₂ fl oz) prepared saffron
(see page 68)

For the couscous:

1 kg (2¹/₄ lb) medium-grain couscous

800 ml (1 pint 7 fl oz) water

1 teaspoon salt

80 g (3 oz) unsalted butter, cut
into pieces

Put the cumin seeds in a small square of muslin and tie it. Stick one clove in each half onion. Season the chicken inside and outside with salt and pepper. In the lower part (stock-pot) of a *couscoussier* (see page 219), put the chicken, add the onion halves, the carrots, cumin seeds and bunch of coriander, season to taste with salt and pepper and cover with the milk. Bring to the boil, then reduce the heat to medium-low and fit the upper part (steamer) in order to steam the couscous as explained on page 115. Leave the chicken and vegetables to cook in the milk for 30 minutes, while steaming the couscous above the stock.

After 30 minutes, add the pumpkin, courgettes and the prepared saffron to the chicken, and continue to cook for 25 minutes.

Check that the chicken is cooked; if not, cook for 5 more minutes. Remove the chicken and cut it into pieces.

To serve, put the couscous in a large, warmed serving dish in a mound with a well in the middle. Put the chicken pieces in the centre and arrange the vegetables around the chicken. Remove and discard the onions, cumin and coriander from the stock and serve the milky stock separately, as a sauce, in a soup tureen.

amfouer

Amfouer is a couscous-like way to use leftover bread. In Morocco, bread was baked at home every day in large quantities and all the leftover bread was kept throughout the week in order to make amfouer on busy days when there was no time for 'real cooking.'

Amfouer is served hot and topped with a cold salad traditionally seasoned with argan oil. Argan oil is made with the fruit of the argan tree, a small stunted tree, on which the goats love to climb and which grows in a very restricted area, south of Agadir. Its oil has a unique flavour and taste and is used mainly with tomato and grilled pepper. It's always used uncooked and usually never mixed with lemon or vinegar. It is produced in an archaic manner and in very small quantities, thus very difficult to find, even in Morocco.

Traditional recipe:

SERVES 6 AS A MAIN COURSE

For the amfouer:

1 1/2 teaspoons paprika

300 ml (1/2 pint) sunflower oil

1.5 litres (2 3/4 pints) cold water

1 kg (2 1/4 lb) stale bread

1 teaspoon salt

1/4 teaspoon Cayenne pepper

1 onion, chopped

For the salad:

4 green peppers

6 large tomatoes, peeled, de-seeded and diced

2 garlic cloves, chopped

1 teaspoon salt

100 ml (3 1/2 fl oz) *argan* oil or olive oil

Preheat the oven to 180°C/350°F/Gas Mark 4.

Put the paprika in a small bowl and cover with the oil; stir with a teaspoon and leave the oil to colour. Pour the water into a large bowl. Cut the stale bread in chunks. Soak the chunks of bread very quickly in cold water, squeeze them thoroughly to remove excess water and crumble them finely in another large bowl until all the bread has been crumbled. Season the bread with the salt, Cayenne pepper and the paprika oil, after stirring the oil. Mix thoroughly with a wooden spoon to impregnate all the bread with the seasonings.

In the upper part of the *couscoussier* (see page 219) put the chopped onion first and then add the seasoned bread. Fill half of the lower part of the *couscoussier* with water and boil it to get it ready for steaming. Prepare the salad before you start steaming the *amfouer*.

Roast the peppers on all sides, in the preheated oven, for 20 minutes, until the skin gets black. Remove from the oven, wrap them in a plastic bag so that they are easier to peel and leave to cool. Once cool, peel them thoroughly and remove the seeds and stalks. Slice them into strips.

In a bowl, put the diced tomato, add the strips of pepper and the chopped garlic and season with salt and *argan* or olive oil, without stirring.

Bring the *couscoussier* to the boil on very high heat. Cook very quickly and remove from the heat 3 minutes after the steam has started getting through the bread. Pour the *amfouer* into a large, deep plate and stir it to mix the onion with the bread. Stir the salad and pour it on top of the *amfouer*. Serve very hot.

Traditional recipe:

SERVES 6 AS A MAIN COURSE

For the spices del'Hsoub:

1/4 teaspoon ground juniper

1/4 teaspoon grated nutmeg

1/4 teaspoon ground mace

1/4 teaspoon ground cinnamon

1/4 teaspoon ground ginger

1/4 teaspoon ground white pepper

1/4 teaspoon ground cloves

1/4 teaspoon ground turmeric

1/4 teaspoon ground cardamom

1/4 teaspoon Cayenne pepper

For the couscous:

150 g (5 1/2 oz) lentils

150 g (5 1/2 oz) dried broad beans

100 g (3 1/2 oz) fresh or dried fenugreek leaves

1 kg (2 1/4 lb) fat beef or lamb meat

mixed spices del'Hsoub (see left)

200 ml (7 fl oz) sunflower oil

4 onions, finely chopped

1 marrow-bone

1 teaspoon salt

2.5 litres (4 1/2 pints) water

1 kg (2 1/4 lb) couscous

couscous
del'Hsoub

Couscous *del'Hsoub* was only served in Morocco, particularly in Casablanca and Marrakech, during exclusive gatherings of Jewish women, who traditionally invited each other to share it once a month. *El'Hsoub* is a secret mix of herbs and spices purportedly invested with aphrodisiac virtues.

The couscous *del'Hsoub* gathering, more than just a lunch, was a unique festive occasion for women to party, sing, dance, laugh and shout the famous joy *youyous*, often accompanied by a band of women musicians and singers: the *chikhats*. Drinking wine and *mahia* (the distilled fig liquor with anise), for the non-Muslims, was an important aspect of the celebration. At tea-time, honeyed pastries and spiced candied fruits were served with mint tea.

In order to make the spices *del'Hsoub*, mix together thoroughly all the spices and keep aside.

Put the lentils in cold water and leave to soak for 4 hours. Put the dried broad beans in cold water and leave to soak for 4 hours. Rinse the fenugreek, clean it, put it in cold water and leave to soak for 3 hours. Sprinkle the meat with half the spices *del'Hsoub* and leave to marinate for 3 hours.

Heat half the oil in a large pan and fry the onions until softened and golden. Add the meat, the marrow-bone, the lentils and the dried broad beans, 1/2 teaspoon salt and the water, bring to the boil and leave to simmer, covered, on medium heat for 45 minutes or until the meat is cooked.

In a bowl, put the couscous, add the fenugreek, the remaining oil and remaining 1/2 teaspoon salt, mix thoroughly and steam the mixture three times, as for other couscous (see method page 115). After the third steaming, pour the mixture into a large bowl, open it up with a wooden spoon, add the second half of the spices *del'Hsoub*. Mix everything together, add salt if necessary and steam for 15 minutes more.

In a large, deep serving platter, put the meat in the centre, surround it with the couscous in the shape of a ring and soak with a ladleful of the meat and onion sauce. Arrange the lentils and broad beans on the couscous and serve very hot.

orange salad
with cinnamon

Traditional recipe:
SERVES 6
6 juicy and seedless oranges
50 g (1³/₄ oz) icing sugar
juice of 1¹/₂ oranges
100 ml (3¹/₂ fl oz) orange-blossom water
To serve:
1 teaspoon ground cinnamon
100 g (3¹/₂ oz) walnuts, coarsely
crushed (optional)
3 mint sprigs

Peel the oranges, remove the pith completely and cut them into slices 5 mm (¹/₄ inch) thick. Discard any pips and core or pith.

Arrange the orange slices on a large, round plate in a spiral shape, each slice slightly overlapping the previous one until the plate is covered completely. Sprinkle on the icing sugar and add the orange juice and the orange-blossom water. Cover with cling film and refrigerate.

Before serving, sprinkle with the ground cinnamon and scatter on the walnuts. Decorate the centre of the plate with the sprigs of mint.

pastilla of pineapple
with a red fruit coulis

Modern recipe:

SERVES 8

2 medium-size pineapples
200 g (7¹/₂ oz) butter
150 g (5¹/₂ oz) caster sugar
8 cloves, ground
4 ouarka sheets (see page 70)
For the coulis:
350 g (12 oz) strawberries, hulled
3 soup spoons icing sugar
juice of 1 lemon

Preheat the oven to 170°C/320°F/Gas Mark 3.

Peel the pineapples, cut them into four lengthways and remove the woody central core. Slice the pineapple quarters in thin slices.

In a deep pan, melt the butter and keep aside 3 tablespoons to brush the *ouarka* sheets later. Then add the sugar, stir well and cook on low heat until the mixture achieves a caramel-like consistency. Add the pineapple slices and cloves. Stir gently to coat everything well with the caramel and cook for 5 minutes on low heat. Leave to cool while draining in a colander.

Brush the entire *ouarka* sheets with melted butter and arrange them on greased baking sheets. Bake for 3 minutes until crisp and golden. Remove from the oven and keep aside while you make the strawberry coulis.

Rinse the strawberries very quickly under running water and process them in a blender. Sieve the coulis while mashing with a wooden spoon and add the icing sugar and lemon juice. Stir and keep aside at room temperature.

On a large serving dish, put a *ouarka* sheet, top gently with the pineapple caramel on the whole surface, add a second *ouarka* sheet, top gently with the pineapple caramel on the whole surface, add a third *ouarka* sheet, top gently with the pineapple caramel on the whole surface, add a fourth *ouarka* sheet, sprinkle with icing sugar and surround the *pastilla* with the strawberry coulis. Serve at once before the *ouarka* sheets get soggy.

Cafe de Ville, Essaouira

couscous seffa

Traditional recipe:

SERVES 4

200 g (7¹/₂ oz) white seedless raisins

1 litre (1³/₄ pints) warm tea

500 g (1 lb 2 oz) medium-grade couscous

800 ml (1 pint 7 fl oz) water

¹/₂ teaspoon salt

80 g (3 oz) unsalted butter,
cut into pieces

80 g (3 oz) icing sugar

100 ml (3¹/₂ fl oz) orange-blossom water

1 tablespoon ground cinnamon

1 litre (1³/₄ pints) buttermilk (optional)

Soak the raisins in the warm tea and leave to swell for an hour. Drain and keep aside.

Steam the couscous as explained on page 115.

Add the sugar, orange-blossom water, three-quarters of the cinnamon and the raisins to the couscous and mix thoroughly. Sprinkle with the remaining cinnamon and serve warm. Serve with buttermilk, if using, in a carafe.

milk pastilla

Traditional recipe:
SERVES 4
For the pastilla:
4 *ouarka* pastry sheets (see page 70)
80 g (3 oz) blanched almonds
(see page 135)
100 ml (3½ fl oz) sunflower oil
10 g (¼ oz) icing sugar
For the kneffa (milk sauce):
400 ml (14 fl oz) milk
80 g (3 oz) icing sugar
1 cinnamon stick
40 ml (1½ fl oz) orange-blossom water
1 tablespoon cornflour

Fold each round pastry sheet in four in a triangular shape. Toast the almonds in a dry frying-pan until golden and crunch them up coarsely.

For the *kneffa*: put aside 2 spoonfuls of milk to dilute the cornflour later. Bring the remaining milk to the boil and add the sugar, the cinnamon and the orange-blossom water. Mix the cornflour into the cold milk and add it to the hot milk. Leave to cook for 2 or 3 minutes stirring well until the mixture starts to thicken. Put the milk through a sieve and leave to cool.

Heat the oil in a deep frying-pan and quickly fry the triangles of *ouarka* (called *pastillas*) until they get evenly golden and crisp. Put them on kitchen paper for excess oil to be absorbed.

Cover the serving plate with *kneffa* (cooked milk sauce). Put a *pastilla* on top of the *kneffa* and sprinkle with the ground almonds and icing sugar.

Clockwise from top left: hand of Fatima, Morocco; Briouats of Almond Paste (page 134); boy carrying baguettes, Kabylie; Milk Pastilla

tart with mroziya

Mroziya can be eaten on its own as a sweet or used to fill tartlets or tarts.

Traditional recipe:
SERVES 8
For the mroziya:
1 kg (2¹/4 lb) seedless black
Malaga raisins
200 g (7 oz) brown cane sugar
2 tablespoons sunflower oil
2 cinnamon sticks
1¹/2 teaspoons ground cinnamon
500 g (1 lb 2 oz) walnut halves
For the tart dough:
200 ml (7 fl oz) sunflower oil
200 ml (7 fl oz) water
1 egg yolk
2 tablespoons sugar
4 tablespoons vanilla sugar
1 tablespoon baking powder
wheat flour

To make the *mroziya*, rinse the raisins quickly under running water. Put them in a large non-stick pan and add all the ingredients, except the walnuts. Bring to the boil, lower the heat to the minimum and let it cook for 1¹/2 hours, stirring often.

Toast the walnuts in a dry pan and coarsely crush two-thirds of them.

The raisins are cooked when the juice has reduced and starts to thicken. Remove the cinnamon sticks and take off the heat, add the crushed walnuts and mix thoroughly. Put the *mroziya* in a serving bowl and decorate with the half-walnuts (if not used as a tart filling). Leave to cool.

Preheat the oven to 180°C/350°F/Gas Mark 4.

To make the dough, mix all the ingredients together in a large bowl. Then add flour slowly to the mixture, stir and keep adding flour and mixing until the dough gets smooth with a soft consistency.

Sprinkle flour on a large board, put aside the equivalent of one egg of dough to decorate the tart and roll the rest of the dough with a rolling pin until it gets to 5 mm (¹/4 inch) thick. Brush a pie plate with oil and line it with the dough sheet.

Put the *mroziya* in a pan on very low heat and heat it slowly for a few minutes while stirring with a wooden spoon. Spread the tart with the filling of *mroziya*. Roll the remaining dough with the rolling pin until it is 3 mm (¹/8 inch) thick and cut it with a jagged pastry wheel in order to get 1 cm (¹/2 inch) wide strips. Criss-cross them on the tart. Put the tart in the preheated oven and cook for 20–30 minutes, until golden. Serve cold, with mint tea (see page 144).

In the afternoon, I had a *hammam* at the Palais Jamai hotel, in Fez. After I was scrubbed and doused with buckets of hot water, I went to the terrace and had a plate of gazelle horns – the delicate biscuits made with almond paste and sugar. Traditionally they are a sign of wealth, being labour-intensive and involving expensive products. They also serve another function. They are always served at Moroccan weddings. Why? I asked a friend. He stared at me in amazement. 'Being horn shaped', he said 'they are natural aphrodisiacs.'

Gazelle horns are shown on page 174.

gazelle horns
Kaab el ghzal

Traditional recipe:

MAKES 35–40

For the almond paste:

250 g (9 oz) blanched almonds (see page 135)

250 g (9 oz) caster sugar

2 small eggs

1/2 teaspoon ground cinnamon

100 ml (3 1/2 fl oz) orange-blossom water

For the dough:

250 g (9 oz) plain flour

1/2 teaspoon salt

3 tablespoons sunflower oil (save 1 spoon to brush the baking tray)

100 ml (3 1/2 fl oz) orange-blossom water

100 ml (3 1/2 fl oz) water

To serve (optional):

100 ml (3 1/2 fl oz) orange-blossom water

75 g (2 3/4 oz) icing sugar

The day before, rinse, drain and dry the blanched almonds with kitchen paper. Spread them on a clean cloth and leave to dry. The almonds must be perfectly dry before you start to make the almond paste.

Preheat the oven to 200°C/400°F/Gas Mark 6. Mince the almonds with a meat mincer or in a food processor. Add the sugar to the almond paste, mix and process the mixture a second time. Then add the 2 whole eggs, the cinnamon and the orange-blossom water. Mix all the ingredients thoroughly into the almond paste. Shape the almond paste with your hands into little curved crescents of about 6 cm (2 1/2 inches) long and 1 cm (1/2 inch) in diameter, with tapering ends, until all the almond paste is used. Leave the little crescents on a plate or small tray brushed with oil as you form them. Set aside.

To make the dough, mix the flour, salt, 2 tablespoons of the oil, orange-blossom water and water together thoroughly. Knead for 10 minutes, into a soft, springy dough. Divide it into balls the size of a small tangerine.

On a lightly floured wooden board, roll out one ball of dough very thinly (about 1 mm) and cut into 7 cm (3-inch) strips. Rotate the board to have the strip horizontally in front of you. Place little almond paste crescents lengthways along a central line on the dough strip, at 3 cm (1 1/2-inch) intervals. Cut the dough at an equal distance between each crescent. Brush the two edges of the dough with a little water and fold over to enclose the almond-paste crescent. With your fingers, press the edges firmly together to seal, following the curved shape of the almond paste filling. Use a jagged pastry cutter to cut away the excess dough.

Put the gazelle horns on a lightly oiled baking tray. Do this very gently to avoid bending them out of shape. Prick each gazelle horn twice with a thin fork. Bake for about 15 minutes, until light golden. Leave to cool and serve plain or lightly sprinkled with orange-blossom water and dusted immediately with icing sugar.

feqquas
with raisins and almonds

Traditional recipe:

MAKES 80-90

150 g (5^1/$_2$ oz) seedless raisins

3 eggs

250 g (9 oz) icing sugar

100 g (3^1/$_2$ oz) unsalted butter,
softened

100 ml (3^1/$_2$ fl oz) sunflower oil

200 g (7^1/$_2$ oz) blanched almonds
(see page 135)

grated zest of ^{1}/$_2$ orange

grated zest of ^{1}/$_2$ lemon

750 g (1 lb 10 oz) wheat flour, sifted

^{1}/$_4$ teaspoon salt

3 tablespoons baking powder

Preheat the oven to 170°C/320°F/Gas Mark 3.
Rinse the raisins, drain them and dry them with
kitchen paper.

In a large bowl, beat the eggs together with
the sugar until you get a pale mixture. Soften the
butter with a wooden spoon until it has a creamy
consistency. Add the oil and the butter to the eggs
and mix. Then add the raisins and almonds and mix
everything thoroughly. Add the orange and lemon
zests to the mixture and stir. Then mix the sifted
flour with the salt and baking powder and add to the
mixture. Knead the dough until it is homogenous.
Shape the dough into regular cylinders of 3.5 cm
(1^3/$_4$ inches) diameter. Set the cylinders of dough
on a baking tray lightly brushed with oil. Bake for
20 minutes.

Remove from the oven before the dough starts
to colour. Cover with a clean cloth and leave to rest
for 3 hours.

Then cut the rolls gently with a sharp knife into
diagonal slices, 4.5 cm (2 inches) long and 4-5 mm
(^{1}/$_4$ inch) thick. Set the slices on a dry baking tray.
Return to the oven and bake for 5-8 minutes until
the slices are evenly golden brown and crisp. Leave
to cool and keep in a biscuit box.

Traditional recipe:

SERVES 12

300 g (10½ oz) walnut halves
1 kg (2¼ lb) caster sugar
400 ml (14 fl oz) water
juice of 2 lemons
½ teaspoon ground gum arabic (optional)
1 small piece (size of 1 chick-pea)
of alum, ground (optional)
5 egg whites

Toast the walnuts, save eight halves and crush the rest coarsely. Keep aside.

Put the sugar in a deep, non-stick pan and add the water. Bring to the boil, lower the heat and leave to cook while stirring in order to make a thick, transparent syrup. Don't leave to become golden. Add the lemon juice, the gum arabic and the alum and remove from the heat. Leave to cool while beating, until warm.

Whisk the egg whites until very thick. Add them to the warm syrup, one spoonful at the time, while stirring with a wooden spoon. *Jabane*'s consistency is like a thick, uncooked meringue. Put the mixture back on very low heat and leave to cook for 5 minutes while stirring. Add the small pieces of walnuts to the *jabane*, avoiding the walnut powder and stir to get them evenly spread in the mixture. Pour the *jabane* into a serving bowl and decorate with the reserved walnut halves. Leave to cool and serve.

jabane

Jabane, a delicious soft nougat, is a popular confectionery in North Africa. The recipe has different variants, as you can add to choice toasted walnuts, almonds, pistachios or even peanuts. North African, and especially Moroccan gastronomy, offers a great variety of nougats which can be soft or hard according to the recipe and made with ginger, sesame seeds, peanuts, flax grains, sunflower seeds, pumpkin seeds or chick-peas. *Jabane* is a tradition of the Moroccan Jewish *Mimouna's* table that celebrates the end of Passover. All Moroccan adults can remember the '*Jabane-man*' who was always standing outside the school doors with what then seemed as a huge white mountain around a long stick. For a few coins, he would tear a large piece of *jabane* off the mountain and sell it to the school kids.

Alum and gum arabic are exotic spices that may be available from North African stores. They are both sold in the form of small 'stones' and have to be ground before use. If they are not available, simply omit them from the recipe.

Briouats of almond paste

Almonds, an essential ingredient in North African cuisine, are used in all kinds of different ways and recipes, throughout the different courses of a meal. As an appetiser, almonds are eaten as part of the *kemia* (see page 154), either steamed with their skin, or grilled in the oven and salted, or blanched, salted and fried. Toasted and crushed, they enhance, flavour and enrich the texture of all kinds of fillings for meat, poultry or fish. Toasted and left whole, they are part of most of the sweet lamb or poultry dishes or sweet couscous.

In pastries, almonds are usually made into a savoury paste, and flavoured, according to the recipe, with orange-blossom water, rose-petal water, lemon zest, orange zest, vanilla or rum (the latter only in the North African Jewish recipes, as the Muslim religion forbids spirits). Almonds are also used in various kinds of nougats, like *jabane* for instance (see page 133). Finally they make a delicious and refreshing drink: the almond milk (see page 143).

Our almond paste recipe can also be used to stuff dried fruits: dates, prunes, apricots, walnuts. In that case, don't use the egg yolk and slightly colour the almond paste to your choice according to the fruits. We find that a pastel pink suits the walnuts, whereas green is best for prunes and yellow for dates (in that case, use the egg yolk). Yellow or green are perfect for apricots.

Briouats of almonds can be folded either in a triangular shape, as in this recipe, or in small rectangles, or in a cigar shape (see page 70). The almond paste freezes very well. The *briouats* also do, provided you freeze them before frying and caramelising.

Briouats of Almond Paste are shown on page 129.

Because of the rose, the wild blackberry is watered.

Arabic proverb

Traditional recipe:

MAKES 48 BRIOUATS

For the almond paste:

250 g (9 oz) blanched almonds (see method)

250 g (9 oz) caster sugar

1 lemon

2 small eggs

100 ml (3½ fl oz) orange-blossom water

For the briouats:

16 *ouarka* sheets (see page 70)

300 ml (½ pint) sunflower oil

75 g (2¾ oz) toasted sesame seeds (optional)

For the syrup:

250 g (9 oz) caster sugar

1 tablespoon clear honey

150 ml (¼ pint) water

juice of 1 lemon

1 tablespoon orange-blossom water

Prepare the almond paste first. If you use almond with skins, blanch them first by plunging them in a large quantity of boiled water. Leave them to swell for 3–5 minutes. Drain and, when cool enough to handle, remove the skin by pinching the almonds between your fingers. Don't leave the almonds to cool too much, or else the skin will dry and stick back to the almonds.

The day before, rinse, drain and dry the blanched almonds with kitchen paper. Spread them on a clean cloth and leave to dry at room temperature. The almonds must be perfectly dry before you mince them. Then mince them with a meat mincer or a food processor. Add the sugar to the almond paste, mix and process the mixture a second time. Grate the lemon zest and add it to the almond paste. Then add the eggs and the orange-blossom water. Thoroughly mix all the ingredients into the almond paste by kneading with your hands. Shape the almond paste into little balls and then flatten them into patties of 3 cm (1½ inches) in diameter and 8 mm (scant ½ inch) thick. Keep aside on a tray brushed with oil.

Then prepare the *briouats*: Cut each *ouarka* sheet in three strips, each of 5 cm (2 inches) wide. Keep one end of the strip straight and cut the other end diagonally. Spread one strip of *ouarka* on your working surface. Put one almond paste patty close to the straight end of the strip and keep on folding in a triangular shape till the end of the paste strip. The triangular parcel thus formed is called *brioua*. To close the *brioua*, slide the diagonal end of *ouarka* into the last slot of the *brioua* (as you would do for an unsealed envelope). Leave the *briouats* on a tray as you make them. Continue in the same manner until you have used all the almond paste and *ouarka*. At this stage you can freeze the *briouats* if you wish to fry them later, by arranging them in a plastic storage container. If you wish to eat them right away, heat the 300 ml (½ pint) sunflower oil in a non-stick pan and fry as many *briouats* as fit in the pan at once, for 2–3 minutes on each side until they get golden and crisp. Drain them on kitchen paper.

Prepare the syrup: put the sugar, honey and water in a heavy-based pan on medium heat and stir with a wooden spoon until the sugar has melted, then lower the heat and leave to simmer for 10 minutes. Add the lemon juice, stir and leave to cook on very low heat for 10 more minutes. Off the heat, add the orange-blossom water and mix with the syrup. For the *briouats*, the syrup must not colour and not be too thick.

Once the *briouats* are fried and cool, dip them in the warm syrup. Remove them with a slotted spoon and arrange them on a serving dish. You can sprinkle toasted sesame seeds on the *briouats* before serving. Serve with mint tea.

kesra
Moroccan bread

Traditional recipe:

MAKES 10 SMALL BREADS

30 g (1¼ oz) fresh yeast

300 ml (½ pint) warm water

1 sugar cube

125 g (4½ oz) unsalted butter

1 kg (2¼ lb) wheat flour

1 teaspoon salt

2 eggs, beaten

1 egg yolk, to glaze

In a bowl, dissolve the yeast with 100 ml (3½ fl oz) of the warm water and one sugar cube and leave it to activate for 20 minutes.

Melt the butter on very low heat without colouring. Set it aside.

Put the flour in a large bowl in a mound with a well in the middle. Put the salt in the centre, add the eggs, the dissolved yeast and the remaining water. Mix thoroughly with your hands. Then add the melted butter and continue to mix gently without kneading in order not to give the dough a rubbery texture.

Divide the dough into 10 equal pieces, shape them into slightly flattened balls and set them on two or three baking trays sprinkled with flour. Cover with a clean cloth and leave to rise for 30–40 minutes at room temperature.

Preheat the oven to 200°C/400°F/Gas Mark 6. Then brush the *kesras* with the egg yolk and bake for 25 minutes until well risen and golden.

The first part of the food ritual is the hand washing ceremony. Before the meal begins, it is customary to exclaim: *Bismillah!* which means 'In the name of God'. This is then followed by the passing of the *kesra*, the bread – usually in a woven basket – which is offered to the guests who will then use their bread as a fork. Most of the dishes are eaten with the hands – only the thumb, index finger and forefinger of the right hand are used. Never use the left hand, which is thought of as unclean.

Bread is crucial. According to Abderrahim Bargache, an expert in Maghrebi cuisine, bread is the most important staple. 'At the table, you must have bread. It is the most important product. If you don't have food, you eat bread and tea.'

Breads, like couscous, vary from region to region: Tangier prefers a grainy bread whilst the Berbers have ten different kinds of loaves. And what is served with it is equally important: at the Royal Cooking School in Rabat, all sorts of relishes served with hot bread: sweet pumpkin; beetroot; tomato and honey; aubergine; cucumber and oregano; and honey, pepper and tomato.

Abdullah Jinjie, who owns a small olive press on the outskirts of Tamesloht, eats hot bread and olive oil for breakfast. He says, 'My wife gets up at 6 am, and bakes four or five loaves of bread a day. I get up at 5 am, go to the *hammam* to wash and then come home and eat my olive oil and bread. Sometimes I have a soup of barley, or *rghaif*, a Moroccan crêpe. But the simple breakfast – bread and olive oil, makes you strong.' He then draws some from the *gave* (jar), dips a small piece of bread into the thick, syrupy stuff and hands it to us. 'A spoonful of olive oil each morning,' he says gravely, 'fortifies male potency.'

Candied fruits or vegetables are very popular in Morocco, particularly among the Jewish community. Always home-made, they usually combine the fruit or vegetable with sugar, spices or aromatic waters. Like all the varieties of biscuits, cookies or small pastries, they are kept at home and served as a sweet after a meal, or together with mint tea, or on special festive meals. Unlike in jams or marmalades, the fruit or vegetable is usually kept entire or cut into large chunks. Carrots, small green tomatoes, pumpkin, courgettes, sweet potatoes, citrons, medlars, clementines, lemons, oranges, grapefruit peels, quinces and figs, can all be candied.

Gum arabic may be available from North African stores. It is sold in the form of little white translucent 'stones', which you need to grind before use. If you can't find it, simply omit it.

candied baby aubergines

Traditional recipe:

1 kg (2^1/$_4$ lb) thin unpeeled baby aubergines 6 cm (2^1/$_2$ inches) long

1 kg (2^1/$_4$ lb) caster sugar

juice of 2 lemons

2 cinnamon sticks

1 teaspoon ground cinnamon

^{1}/$_2$ teaspoon ground cloves

^{1}/$_2$ teaspoon freshly grated root ginger

^{1}/$_2$ teaspoon ground mace

^{1}/$_2$ teaspoon grated nutmeg

^{1}/$_2$ teaspoon ground gum arabic (optional)

500 ml (18 fl oz) water

Choose very small, dark and hard aubergines. Rinse them under running water, remove the leaves and leave the entire stalk. Prick them with a fork and steam them for 15 minutes. Drain them and leave them to cool while draining.

Put the sugar, the lemon juice and all the spices in a deep non-stick pan and add the water. Bring to the boil, lower the heat and leave to cook for 10 minutes while stirring, in order to make a syrup.

Squeeze the aubergines gently in your hand to remove excess water and put them in the syrup. Cook on a very low heat for 1^1/$_4$ hours, checking the syrup level occasionally. Remove from the heat and leave to cool. Arrange the aubergines attractively on the serving dish with the stalks upwards (in French this presentation is called *en buisson* or 'in a bush').

Candied aubergines keep very well in a jar.

candied grapefruit peel

Traditional recipe:

2 kg (4^1/$_2$ lb) grapefruits with very
thick peel
2 kg (4^1/$_2$ lb) caster sugar
juice of 2 lemons
500 ml (18 fl oz) water
200 ml (7 fl oz) orange-blossom water

Rinse the grapefruits and dry them with kitchen paper. Grate and discard the zest and quarter them (or more according to size). Remove core, pith and pips. Cover the flesh with water in a large bowl and leave to soak for 2 days, changing the water four times a day.

The third day, put in a large pan, cover with water and bring to the boil. Keep boiling for 15 minutes. Then drain the fruits and discard the cooking water. Repeat this operation twice. Leave to cool, remove and discard the flesh. Drain the grapefruit peel thoroughly and keep aside.

In a large deep pan, put the sugar and the lemon juice and add the water, bring to the boil, lower the heat, stir and leave cook slowly for 15 minutes in order to make a syrup.

Put the quartered grapefruit peel in the syrup. Bring to the boil, lower the heat and leave to cook on medium heat for 1 hour, checking the syrup level and stirring occasionally. The syrup must be thick and the peel clear and transparent. Add the orange-blossom water and boil for 1 minute. Remove from the heat, leave to cool and keep in jars. Close the jars only when perfectly cold.

The same recipe applies to orange, lemon and bitter orange peels.

2 kg (4½ lb) large lemons with very thick peel
1 kg (2¼ lb) coarse salt
100 ml (3½ fl oz) sunflower oil

pickled lemons

Aicha Hamiani, the director of the Royal Cooking School in Rabat says: 'In my father's garden in Fez there is the most beautiful tree. And a very unusual tree, because it produces lemons. But not large, round yellow lemons like you see every day. No, these are special small juicy lemons which we use here, preserved with salt. They are small, the size of large olives and only the skin is eaten, not the inside. They have a taste unlike any other – you can tell the minute you eat one that you are eating the lemon from my father's tree. And,' she adds, 'once you have tasted my father's lemons, it would be an insult for you to have a dish prepared with regular lemons'.

Pickled or preserved lemon is an ingredient of the utmost importance in the Moroccan cuisine as it is essential to many typical dishes, served hot like Chicken *Tagine* with Olives and Pickled Lemon (page 108), Sea Bass *Tagine* with Potatoes (page 84), or cold like *Merk Hzina* Salad (page 65). Pickled lemons are very easy to make at home and far better than when bought from the shop. In Morocco, Tunisia and Algeria, the pickles stores display huge domes of pickled lemons, dozens of varieties of olives and pickled peppers and mountains of *harissa* (see recipe for *sahka*, page 59). Pickled lemons can be made with very small lemons with thin peel, the size of a small apricot (difficult to find in Europe), or with very large lemons with thick peel. Pickled lemons are rinsed and dried with kitchen paper before use, their flesh is removed and discarded and the peel is used in large strips in the *tagines* or small pieces in the salads.

In Tunisia, there is a very tasty relish made with chopped pickled lemon, *harissa*, crushed garlic and a little olive oil.

Wash the lemons thoroughly under running water and cut off their two ends. With a sharp knife, cut each lemon lengthways stopping 1.5 cm (⅝ inch) before the end in order to keep the halves attached. Turn the lemon upside-down and rotate it in order to cross cut it in half lengthways on the other side, again stopping 1.5 cm (⅝ inch) before the bottom. You should obtain four attached quarters. Prepare a large clean jar. Hold each lemon vertically, open it by squeezing it slightly without detaching the two parts and stuff it with coarse salt. Close it with your hand to keep the salt inside and turn it upside-down to stuff the other side with coarse salt. Put the lemon in the jar and continue with the remaining lemons, stacking them one on the other until the jar is full. Tamp the lemons down as much as you can and add a heavy clean stone wrapped in cling film on the top.

The lemons will produce juice every day and should be completely covered with juice after the third or fourth day. When they are covered, shake the jar two or three times to stir the juice, pour the oil on the surface of the jar in order to prevent mould (which is harmless and pickled lemons are always rinsed before use) and leave in a cool place. After 3 weeks you can start using the pickled lemons.

Fez

Traditional recipe:

SERVES 12

1 kg (2¼ lb) juicy lemons

2 litres (3½ pints) water

500 g (1 lb 2 oz) caster sugar

2 vanilla pods

To serve:

12–24 ice cubes

12 sprigs of fresh mint

agua limon

Fresh lemon juice drinks are very popular in Morocco, Algeria and Tunisia. The method of the recipe and the flavouring (vanilla, rose-petal water, orange-blossom water, fresh mint leaves) may slightly vary from one country to the other or from one recipe to the other but the basic ingredients are always the same: lemon, sugar and water. Chilled lemon juice is made at home and also served in any cafe or street corner.

Wash the lemons thoroughly, cut them in half and squeeze them. Strain the juice and put it aside in the fridge.

Take the lemon peels, cut off each little end and grind them (zest, pith and flesh) in a meat-mincer or food processor. Put them in a large bowl, pour over 1 litre (1¾ pints) of the water, cover the bowl with cling film and leave to soak overnight in the fridge.

Put the sugar and vanilla pods in a deep, non-stick pan and add the remaining 1 litre (1¾ pints) water. Bring to the boil, lower the heat and leave to cook for 10 minutes while stirring, in order to make a thin, transparent syrup. Don't leave to become golden. Remove from heat and leave to cool. Strain to remove the vanilla pods before using.

Strain the ground lemon peels, keep the juice and discard the peels. In a large bowl, add the lemon juice, the strained vanilla syrup and the peel juice. Stir, cover with cling film and refrigerate.

Stir again before serving. Put 1 or 2 ice cubes in each large glass, pour on the *agua limon* and decorate with a sprig of fresh mint.

almond milk

Traditional recipe:

SERVES 12

400 g (14 oz) caster sugar

400 g (14 oz) blanched almonds
(see page 135)

1 litre (1³/₄ pints) water

2 litres (3¹/₂ pints) non-skimmed milk

1 cinnamon stick

200 ml (7 fl oz) orange-blossom water

To serve:

12–24 ice cubes

¹/₄ teaspoon ground cinnamon

Add 200 g (7 oz) of the sugar to the almonds and grind them at length and very finely in a food processor. Put them in a large bowl, pour over the water and stir. Cover the bowl with cling film and leave to soak for a whole night in the fridge. Pour the milk into a deep pan, add the remaining 200 g (7 oz) sugar and the cinnamon stick and bring to the boil while stirring. Remove from the heat and leave to cool. Skim, remove the cinnamon stick, add the orange-blossom water and stir.

Stir the almonds in their soaking juice before straining them while squeezing thoroughly with a wooden spoon in order to extract all the juice; add the almond juice to the milk. Discard the almonds or use them in another recipe. Cover the mixture with cling film and refrigerate.

Stir again before serving. Put 1 or 2 ice cubes in each large glass, pour over the almond milk and sprinkle, to taste, a pinch of ground cinnamon on each glass.

mint tea

Traditional recipe:

SERVES 6

large bunch of spearmint (or your choice of mints)

1¹/2 teaspoons Chinese green tea

6 teaspoons sugar

In the last 150 years mint tea has become an integral part of the North African culture and the first sign of welcome at any social level. The teapots have a specific shape and range from the one-glass size to up to 12- or even 16-glass size. Traditionally plain and made with a mixed pewter, the older and best ones had the famous fly stamped in the bottom. Today some pale and heavier copies are sold, so the fly sign is no longer a guarantee of quality.

Mint tea is traditionally served in a slightly slanted glass either plain transparent or richly decorated with bright green, red or blue colours highlighted with golden motifs. Never in a cup. It is a habit not to fill the glass completely and to pour the tea from very high in order to form a foam of large bubbles on the surface. A legend says that the higher the servant can lift the teapot to pour the tea into the glass, the better it is for the class, reputation and good taste of the host, as his guests, sitting on low sofas, could see the famous and very chic *Made in England* engraved on the bottom of the teapots.

Mint tea is always made with Chinese green tea, the most popular brand being the famous gunpowder green tea sold in deep green boxes of all sizes. Mint tea is always sugared in the teapot, using usually chunks of sugar loaf. In Morocco if you look the least like a potential client to a shop tender, you will be offered a glass of mint tea to hold you longer into the shop, particularly in the carpet or the craft shops in the *souks*. Mint tea is made with fresh mint leaves and Morocco grows all kinds of varieties. Moroccans add more fresh mint leaves in the glass and Tunisians sprinkle some toasted pine seeds in the glass.

Boil the water and rinse the teapot. Then leave boiling water in the teapot to heat it while you prepare the tea. Rinse the bunch of mint quickly under running water and shake it to remove excess water. Cut off the bottom of the stems. Empty the teapot and put in the tea, rinse it quickly with a little boiling water and throw the water away, leaving the tea leaves. (This initial rinsing removes some of the bitterness of the tea leaves.) Bring the water to the boil again. Twist the mint leaves and remaining stems in your hands before putting them in the teapot, it will allow the mint aromas to better spread in the tea. Add the mint and the sugar and pour the boiling water into the teapot making sure that you cover all the mint with boiling water. If not, the leaves that don't soak will turn black with the steam and give a very bad taste to the tea. Leave to brew for 3 minutes. Don't brew the tea for too long as it becomes dark and bitter.

Stir everything inside the teapot with a long spoon. Pour in one glass then return the contents of the glass to the teapot. This method allows a better mixture of the ingredients. Then pour the tea into six glasses, as explained in the introduction. Mint tea is drunk very hot, that's why Moroccans sip it noisily.

In many ways Tunisians eat like Italians: they love their food. They love its visual appeal, its sensuality, its aphrodisiac qualities and the contrast between sweet and savoury. I realised this one wintry day in Paris in the Belleville section where there is a heavy concentration of North African families. Shop after shop specialises in Tunisian, Algerian or Moroccan food: here you can buy Chinese gunpowder tea (which is essential for making mint tea), bottles of Selecto (the Algerian version of Coca Cola), or Boga (the Tunisian version of the same).

At one tiny restaurant, Chez René et Gabin (*'Le Numéro Un du Casse Croûte Tunisien'* – *casse croûte tunisien* is the famous overstuffed sandwich which Tunisians love) people crowded inside and ordered specialities that they had eaten at home in Tunisia. There was *minina*, an omelette made with potatoes and eggs and then sliced cold and eaten like a cake; *mlokheyia*, a thick, strongly flavoured blackish-green sauce made from *corete* powder, garlic, spices and olive oil, which was served over *merguez*, sausages or chunks of beef; and a Tunisian version of couscous, made with fish – a recipe that comes from the city of Sfax.

All of this was eaten with glasses of red wine. The wine was *casher* (kosher) because the restaurant is Jewish. But it was not the fact of what they were eating that struck me, it was the way these people, all Tunisian emigrés, were eating: with pure joy and a strong desire to be sitting at those simple tables and tasting the food. ✦

Tunisia

TUNISIAN FOOD

Tunisia, like Algeria and Morocco, is a mélange of cultures. Throughout its history, Tunisia has been invaded: the Arabs arrived in the seventh century, the Ottomans in the sixteenth century and the French followed in the nineteenth century.

All three left an indelible stamp on the country, the culture and especially the cuisine; however the two major influences on the cuisine are Italian and Jewish. There are shops specialising in Italian food, such as *ravioli con ricotta*, spaghettini and macaroni to be used for pasta with shellfish.

Bread in Tunisia is exquisite and so plentiful. The aroma of *le pain de maison* wafting through the streets of Tunis in the early morning, is one of the most characteristic smells of Tunisia.

The most famous Tunisian condiment is *harissa*, which is made from chillies, garlic, caraway and salt. Even if you order a simple tuna salad in Tunisia, it arrives with a serving of *harissa* on the side. The *harissa* is usually seasoned with freshly chopped onion and parsley and generously soaked with olive oil; most people use it in an unabashed fashion.

Like the Algerians, the Tunisians are fond of Turkish-inspired *briks*. There are many versions of *briks* – some of the most popular are *Brik maison au thon à l'huile* (with tinned tuna fish), or *brik maison au poulet* (with chicken).

Soups, thick and spicy, are important. I have eaten a Tunisian speciality, a rich soup of chick-peas, but there are equally light and refreshing versions, such as a vegetable and egg soup.

In the beautiful coastal city of Sfax, fishermen bring their daily catch back to the port in long wooden boxes, much in the same way they did at the beginning of the century and display them to vendors. *'Acheter le poisson à Sfax est un art'* ('buying fish in Sfax is an art'), writes Mohamad Masmoudi, who has written a tribute to that city.

Finally, there is couscous, the national dish. It comes in a variety of forms with chicken, lamb offal, fish or beef. Couscous made with fish and red sauce is a speciality of Sfax where some families eat it up to three times a week. When the couscous comes layered, Jerba-style, it is known as *masfouf*. The sweet version of *masfouf*, made with raisins, nuts, sugar and seedless grapes is a traditional way of breaking the *ramadan* fast.

A Bedouin with his *sloughi*, the hunting dog of his people

JEWISH FOOD

The history of Jewish food echoes the history of the Jewish people. By the beginning of the nineteenth century, there were roughly 50,000 Jews living in Tunisia, largely along the coast in Nabeul, Sousse, Mahdiya, Sfax, Gabes and Djerba. In the interior, they lived mainly in Kef, Gafsa and Nefta. Many became merchants or jewellers.

When they arrived in the new country, they brought their food, traditions and their own style of cooking which complied with their religious laws. These recipes have been passed on from family to family.

Cooking is forbidden on the *Shabbat* and so the *dafina* – the one-meal Saturday dish – was developed. The recipe is handed down from generation to generation and varies depending on whether one is in Tunis or in Casablanca, but whatever the recipe the method is the same. Traditionally the cook shops and combines the ingredients before the *Shabbat* and then, usually on late Friday afternoon before sunset, takes the clay pot to a neighbourhood baker where the dish is slow-cooked in a vast oven. On Saturday at noon, after prayers at Synagogue, the *dafina* is proudly carried home. A shopkeeper from rue Charbonnier in Paris (a Mecca for Tunisian emigrés) told me his family *dafina* is made with courgettes and yams.

Veal, lamb or beef are the preferred Jewish meats, but there are variations. Pork is *never* used and the same goes for shellfish. While a *tagine de veau aux zitoun* (veal with olives) may be popular with Moroccan Jews, the Tunisian Jews from the Jewish quarter of Djerba might serve *bkaila* (okra with lamb or beef) and Algerian Jews might serve *coclo* (big meatballs made of minced beef, rice and spices), which might either be served alone, or alongside a *dafina*.

JEWISH HOLIDAY DISHES

There are several important holidays in which food plays a large part. *Rosh Hashanah*, the high holy day that marks the beginning of the Jewish New Year, usually falls in September or October, depending on the lunar calendar. Rich festive meals are prepared. As with all Jewish holidays, each family has their own traditions, but there are special religious customs such as dipping apples in honey which guarantee a sweet year. Certain holiday foods have symbolic meaning for Jews throughout the world, whether they are *ashkenaze* or *sepharade*.

Yom Kippur, the holiest day of the Jewish year, is a day of abstinence and fasting from the afternoon of one day until the following evening of the next day. The fast is usually broken by all kinds of pastries and meals that have been prepared in advance.

Inquire about the mother before you marry a girl.

Arabic proverb

Finally there is Passover (*Pessah*), the eight-day season that commemorates the Jews escaping from Egypt. At Passover only unleavened bread (*matzots*) can be eaten. On the first two nights a vast meal is prepared for the *sedder* table, usually involving lamb, fresh broad beans and a soup of chicken and mint, or *marag l'hamd* (a sour soup made with lemon juice and beef bones). The *harosset* is a delicacy made with dates and served during the *sedder*. It is a paste made with dates, walnuts, almonds and dried figs, kneaded together with grape juice or sweet red wine. It symbolises the cement that the Jewish slaves used to seal the stones of the pyramids in Egypt. Each North African country has its own variant of the basic recipe: in Constantine (Algeria), a mashed pomegranate is added, in Tetouan (Northern Morocco), a grated apple and a pinch of pepper is added and in Setif (Tunisia), a ground rose blossom is added.

This recipe is the Tunisian version of *tchaktchouka* which is a very popular dish in the three North African countries. It is served either cold or hot. When cold it is eaten, with bread, as a cooked salad. Hot, it can be served with spicy sausages called *merguez*, with little meatballs cooked in the *tchaktchouka*, with preserved meat (*khlii*), with scrambled eggs mixed into the *tchaktchouka*, or with all kinds of vegetables: aubergines, broad beans, potatoes, artichokes, peas. The Jewish Moroccan version of *tchaktchouka*, called *metboukha* (meaning 'cooked'), includes peeled tomatoes, grilled green peppers, garlic, paprika, Cayenne pepper or chilli, green chillies and sunflower oil. It is cooked at length until it becomes like a deep red *confit* marmalade and served cold as an appetiser in little home-made salty tartlets, called *barquettes* or on small croûtons made of toasted slices of thin baguette (like Italian *crostini*) or served hot with fried eggs on top. Either way *tchaktchouka* is delicious and a good multi-purpose base to keep in the fridge for 4 or 5 days. *Tchaktchouka* freezes perfectly.

tchaktchouka
in the Tunisian style

Traditional recipe:

SERVES 8 AS A STARTER OR SALAD

100 ml (3 1/2 fl oz) olive oil
3 onions, finely chopped
6 garlic cloves, crushed
4 green peppers, de-seeded
and chopped
1 kg (2 1/4 lb) unpeeled tomatoes,
de-seeded and diced
1 teaspoon salt
1/2 teaspoon ground white pepper
1/4 teaspoon ground caraway
1/2 teaspoon ground coriander
1/2 teaspoon dried mint

Heat the olive oil in a large, non-stick pan. Add the chopped onions and crushed garlic and fry on low heat until golden. Add the chopped peppers and continue to fry while stirring for 5 minutes. Then add the diced tomatoes with salt and pepper. Cover the pan and leave to cook for 1 hour, checking and stirring occasionally.

After 45 minutes, uncover the pan, raise the heat and let the remaining liquid evaporate, keeping an eye on it to prevent it from sticking.

After the last 15 minutes, turn the heat off, add the caraway, coriander and dried mint, stir, cover and leave to infuse for 15 minutes before serving. This will allow the spices to spread their aromas into the *tchaktchouka*.

fresh broad bean salad

Traditional recipe:

SERVES 4 AS A STARTER OR SALAD

1.25 kg (2³/4 lb) fresh or 500 g
(1 lb 2 oz) frozen broad beans
2 litres (3¹/2 pints) water
1 teaspoon salt
100 ml (3¹/2 fl oz) olive oil
1 onion, finely chopped
³/4 pickled lemon (see page 141),
flesh discarded, peel chopped
¹/4 teaspoon ground white pepper
1 teaspoon ground cumin
2 tablespoons chopped fresh coriander,
to garnish

This recipe uses fresh broad beans without their pods. Out of season, frozen broad beans may be used. If fresh, remove the pods. Boil the 2 litres (3¹/2 pints) of water with the salt. Add the broad beans, bring to the boil again and cook for 3–4 minutes. Then immediately run cold water over the beans to preserve their bright green colour. Once cool, remove their outermost skins by pinching them between your fingers.

Heat the oil in a pan and fry the onion slowly until slightly golden. Add the beans, chopped pickled lemon and pepper. Stir and let the mixture cook gently for 5 more minutes. Halfway through the cooking, add the cumin. Serve warm after having sprinkled on the fresh coriander.

Fresh broad beans are very commonly used throughout North Africa, either with their pods as a vegetable with fish or meat, or with other vegetables in the couscous stock, or in cooked salads, usually seasoned with cumin, lemon juice and olive oil. Steamed fresh beans without the pods are an excellent appetiser, just seasoned with salt and ground cumin. Dried broad beans are either fried, salted and eaten as an appetiser, just like peanuts or almonds, or used as the main ingredient in a spicy thick soup with cumin and paprika (*bessara*).

Broad beans, steamed or fried, are usually part of the huge appetiser table: the traditional *kemia*, very popular throughout North Africa. *Kemia* is the equivalent of *tapas* in Spain or *zakouski* in Russia. It varies from one country to the other. The Tunisians will most often put smoked dried fish eggs (the *boutargue*), potato salad with *harissa*, pickled turnips, steamed fresh almonds, *mechouia* (see page 62) and *minina*. The Moroccans will include a huge variety of olives: purple, green and black olives, seasoned with garlic, red pepper and fresh coriander, dried salted black olives, cracked bitter green olives, large green olives with pickled lemons, pickled vegetables and pickled green chillies, *briouats* and spicy cigars (see page 70), varieties of salted nuts including fried chick-peas, steamed white truffles with salt and cumin and small liver balls in *chermoula* (see page 80). Algerians will serve little spicy sausages (the *merguez*), cold *tchaktchouka*, bite-size *keftas*, radishes, raw artichokes and lots of cooked salads.

squid in red sauce with herbs and spices

Traditional recipe:

SERVES 4 AS A MAIN COURSE

1 kg (2^1/$_4$ lb) medium-size squid

For the sauce:

3 tablespoons olive oil

1 onion, finely chopped

3 garlic cloves, crushed

2 tablespoons concentrated tomato purée

300 ml (^{1}/$_2$ pint) water

1 thyme sprig

1 bay leaf

^{1}/$_2$ pickled lemon, chopped

1 teaspoon salt

^{1}/$_4$ teaspoon ground white pepper

juice of 2 lemons

^{1}/$_2$ tablespoon *harissa* (see page 148)

1 teaspoon ground cumin

Clean and wash the squid and cut them in 2 cm (^{3}/$_4$-inch) slices. Heat the oil and fry the onions and garlic until golden. Dilute the tomato purée in 50 ml/2 fl oz of the water. To the onion pan, add the tomato purée, then all the other ingredients, except the cumin. Bring to the boil. Add the squid, lower the heat and leave to cook for 25 minutes. After 15 minutes, add the cumin, stir, raise the heat and keep cooking, uncovered for 10 minutes. Serve hot, with white rice.

tuna and egg brik

Briks are the Tunisian version of the Moroccan *briouats* or the Algerian *boureks*. They use the same pastry sheet, called *malsouqua* in Tunisia, but are shaped differently. One of the most traditional *brik* recipes is the one with tuna and egg that we give here. *Briks* can also be stuffed with *tchaktchouka* (see page 153) or potatoes. *Briks* normally use the entire pastry sheet and are folded in half in a semi-circular shape, more or less like a *pizza calzone* or even a British pasty.

Traditional recipe:
SERVES 4
150 g (5¹/₂ oz) tuna tinned in oil
2 tablespoons olive oil
2 onions, minced
6 tablespoons finely chopped fresh flat-leaved parsley
¹/₂ teaspoon salt
¹/₂ teaspoon ground white pepper
300 ml (¹/₂ pint) sunflower oil
4 *malsouqua* or *ouarka* (see page 70) pastry sheets
1 egg white, beaten
1 lemon, quartered, to serve

Drain the tuna from its oil. Heat the olive oil in a non-stick frying-pan, add the onion and parsley and leave to cook for 6–7 minutes on very low heat while stirring until softened and translucent. Off the heat, add the tuna and mix thoroughly with a wooden spoon to obtain a homogeneous paste. Season to taste with salt and pepper.

Heat the oil for deep-frying. Quickly lay a pastry sheet on an oil-brushed plate. Fold it in two with the round edges towards you, just to mark the half and then re-open it. Put two large spoonfuls of the tuna filling on the lower half, dig a little well in the filling and then carefully break an egg in the well. Season with salt and pepper, fold the pastry sheet over again and seal the round side, 2 cm (³/₄ inch) from the edge, by pressing strongly with your fingers in order to trap all the stuffing inside. For better sealing, you can brush the surround with egg white.

Immediately slide the *brik* carefully into the hot oil and deep-fry until golden on both sides. Scoop out with a large wooden spoon, draining the oil as much as you can. Serve at once, with a lemon quarter to squeeze over.

tagine of mussels *with fennel and peas*

Traditional recipe:

SERVES 6 AS A MAIN COURSE

2 kg (4^1/$_2$ lb) live mussels

50 g (1^3/$_4$ oz) unsalted butter

2 onions, chopped

^{1}/$_2$ teaspoon ground white pepper

500 g (1 lb 2 oz) fennel bulbs

1.5 litres (2^3/$_4$ pints) water

1 teaspoon salt

150 ml (^{1}/$_4$ pint) olive oil

2 garlic cloves, crushed

2 celery sticks, chopped

3 large tomatoes, skinned, de-seeded and finely chopped

100 g (3^1/$_2$ oz) peas

1 large green pepper, de-seeded and cut into large strips

1 large yellow pepper, de-seeded and cut into large strips

1 large red pepper, de-seeded and cut into large strips

2 tablespoons chopped fresh coriander, to garnish

Wash and thoroughly scrape the mussels under running water.

In a large pan, heat the butter and half the chopped onions. Add half the ground white pepper and cook for 3 minutes until the onions are translucent. Add the mussels and cover the pan. Leave to cook for 2–3 minutes until all the mussels are opened. Take the pan from the heat and remove the mussels from their shells. Discard all the mussels that did not open. Keep the mussels aside. Strain the cooking juice and keep aside in a bowl.

Wash and clean the fennel bulbs, remove the hard parts and cut into thick slices, lengthways. Cook the fennel in boiling, salted water with a tablespoon of the olive oil added for 10 minutes. Leave them a little hard so as to finish the cooking later.

In the *tagine* plate, heat the remaining olive oil, add the garlic, the celery and the remaining onion and fry for 1 minute. Then add the tomatoes, peas, peppers and fennel. Add the remaining ground pepper and 6 tablespoons of the mussel cooking juice. Leave to cook, covered, for 10–12 minutes, at a gentle simmer. Uncover, raise the heat and leave any excess water to evaporate for 3 minutes. Add the mussels and cook, uncovered, for 1 more minute. Finally, scatter the chopped coriander on the dish, cover the *tagine* and serve immediately.

Clockwise from top left: freshly caught mussels for sale; fishing at Mahdin, Tunisia; Tagine of Mussels with Fennel and Peas; fish seller at Tunis central market

tagine mqualli
of beef and fennel

Traditional recipe:

SERVES 4 AS A MAIN COURSE

1.25 kg (2³/₄ lb) boneless beef shin

100 ml (3¹/₂ fl oz) sunflower oil

1 teaspoon salt

¹/₂ teaspoon ground white pepper

1 teaspoon ground ginger

100 ml (3¹/₂ fl oz) prepared saffron
(see page 68)

2 garlic cloves, finely crushed

4 large fennel bulbs

juice of 1¹/₂ lemons

1 teaspoon wheat flour

150 g (5¹/₂ oz) green olives, stoned

1 pickled lemon, cut into strips
(see page 141)

2 tablespoons chopped fresh coriander,
to garnish

Cut the beef shin in eight slices of 1.5 cm (⁵/₈ inch) thick. In a large saucepan, heat the oil and fry the meat slices gently on both sides. Add the salt, pepper, ground ginger, prepared saffron and crushed garlic. Add water to cover and bring to the boil, lower the heat and leave to cook, covered, for 45 minutes.

Clean the fennel bulbs, removing all the hard parts, wash and cut into thick slices, lengthways. Leave the fennel in cold water with 2 tablespoons of lemon juice added until needed.

After 45 minutes, remove the meat slices and keep aside on a plate. Drain the fennel from its soaking water, add the remaining lemon juice and the fennel slices to the cooking juice, cover and leave to cook on low heat for 40 minutes. Remove the fennel slices and keep aside. Add the flour to the sauce and stir. Then add the olives and strips of pickled lemon, raise the heat and leave to cook for 5 minutes until the sauce has reduced and thickened, stirring occasionally. In a large *tagine* plate, put the meat slices in the centre in overlapping layers. Arrange the fennel slices in a ring shape around the meat. Pour the cooking juice with olives and pickled lemon on top of the meat and fennel. Cover the *tagine* and return to cook for 5 minutes on low heat. Sprinkle with fresh coriander and serve hot.

sautéed prawns in an oriental style

Traditional recipe:

SERVES 4 AS A MAIN COURSE

300 ml (1/2 pint) olive oil

5 garlic cloves, finely crushed

3 dried *piments de Cayenne* peppers, or other small, very hot, dried chillies, finely crushed (including seeds)

800 g (1 3/4 lb) medium-size raw prawns, shelled

2 tablespoons paprika

1 teaspoon salt

3 tablespoons finely chopped fresh flat-leaved parsley

Heat the oil in a large *tagine* plate. When very hot, add the garlic and crushed Cayenne peppers. Fry for 1 minute. Add the prawns and paprika and stir-fry for 3 minutes, on high heat. Sprinkle with the salt and parsley and serve, uncovered, and still sizzling.

dafina

Dafina (also called *T'fina* or *Skheena*) is the traditional Saturday lunch meal (*Shabbat*) in North African Jewish families. All of the North African cultures have their own style of Jewish cooking which is important to their culture, and the influence is particularly strong in Morocco and Tunisia. Tunisian Jews, in particular, have a strong desire to retain their identity and their cultural roots. You can be sitting in an oceanfront Haifa restaurant looking out over the Mediterranean, or sitting in a crowded cafe like *Chez René et Gabin* on the Boulevard de Belleville in Paris, and you will find homesick Tunisians who have exported their Jewish specialities, such as *dafina kamounia* (with white beans and cumin), *dafina bkaila* (with a dark green tasty sauce), and *dafina nikitouche* (with very small round pasta).

Dafina cooks very slowly from Friday evening to Saturday lunch-time, usually for 18–20 hours. The Jewish religion forbids cooking during *Shabbat*, thus the invention of *dafina* in order to be able to still get a hot meal on *Shabbat*. It has lots of variants (with wheat, sweet stuffing, dried beans instead of chick-peas, calves' foot, etc.). It is a very social dish that gathers a great number of people around the table. In Morocco, it was traditionally sent to cook in the local public oven. Today, the cooking takes place at home either in a very low electric oven, or on an electric plate where the pan is covered with a heavy wool blanket, dedicated to that specific use. Cooking *dafina* is like gambling as, due to the fact that the heat cannot be modified, one never knows if the result will be a dark golden brown roasted dish or an almost pale and boiled stew, disaster that could ruin the *Shabbat* lunch. The only possible control is to add water during the night if evaporation is too quick.

To cope with the heaviness of the dish, *dafina* is usually served with *mahia*, a white distilled liquor of figs and anise. The typical town or village clown, *bambara*, was usually a very tall and black man from the Sudan, always carrying his monkey sitting on his shoulder. On Saturday afternoons, he used to come to the Jewish district called the *mellah* and ask his monkey to show everybody what the typical Jew does on Saturday afternoon after he had *dafina* with *mahia*. The monkey would then lie on his back and start snoring.

Traditional recipe:

SERVES 8 AS A MAIN COURSE

200 g (7 oz) chick-peas

24 small potatoes, peeled

1 calves' foot, cut into 4 pieces

500 g (1 lb 2 oz) shin of beef

2 stoned dates

400 g (14 oz) long-grain rice

450 ml (^{3}/$_4$ pint) sunflower oil

2^1/$_2$ teaspoons salt

2 teaspoons ground white pepper

^{3}/$_4$ teaspoon ground turmeric

400 g (14 oz) wheat grains (or spelt)

2 pinches of Cayenne pepper

1 teaspoon paprika

4 unpeeled garlic cloves

400 g (14 oz) minced beef

2 tablespoons brown breadcrumbs

1 egg (for the stuffing)

1 tablespoon caster sugar

^{1}/$_2$ teaspoon ground cinnamon

1 teaspoon meatball spices
(see page 93)

100 ml (3^1/$_2$ fl oz) water

8 uncooked eggs in their shells

ground cumin, to serve

hot paprika, to serve

The day before, soak the chick-peas in cold water.

The next day, in a very large and deep pan, put the chick-peas, the potatoes, the pieces of calves' foot, the entire piece of beef shin and the dates.

Rinse the rice and put it in a bowl with 4 tablespoons of the oil, ^{1}/$_2$ teaspoon salt, ^{1}/$_2$ teaspoon pepper and ^{1}/$_4$ teaspoon turmeric. Mix everything together and pour the mixture into a sealed greaseproof paper bag, large enough to contain two-and-a-half times the volume of the rice. Add the rice bag to the pan.

Rinse the wheat grains and put in a bowl with 4 tablespoons of the oil, ^{1}/$_2$ teaspoon salt, ^{1}/$_2$ teaspoon pepper, the Cayenne pepper, paprika and the unpeeled garlic cloves. Mix everything together and pour the mixture into a sealed greaseproof paper bag, large enough to contain two-and-a-half times the volume of the wheat. Add the wheat bag to the pan.

In a bowl, put the minced meat and add the brown breadcrumbs, ^{1}/$_2$ teaspoon salt, ^{1}/$_2$ teaspoon pepper, the entire raw egg, 2 tablespoons of the oil, the caster sugar, cinnamon, meatball spices and water and mix everything together very thoroughly. Roll this stuffing in cling film in the shape of an 8 cm (3-inch) thick sausage. Add the wrapped stuffing to the pan.

Sprinkle 1 teaspoon salt, ^{1}/$_2$ teaspoon of pepper and ^{1}/$_2$ teaspoon of turmeric into the pan. Add 200 ml (7 fl oz) of the oil. Rinse the 8 raw eggs and add them very carefully on top of everything else. Cover with water and bring to the boil; cook on high heat for 1 hour. Add water if necessary after 1 hour to cover again and cook, covered, on a very low heat for between 18 and 20 hours.

Serving *dafina* is an art as everything is served hot in separate dishes. Sometimes they are eaten with ground cumin or hot pepper to taste.

The first thing to do is to shell the eggs and quickly return them to the pan to keep them hot.

The potatoes and the eggs are served together, whole, in the same plate, with a little cooking juice added. The wheat, the rice and the meat stuffing are removed from their wrappings and set in three separate dishes after the stuffing has been sliced. The piece of beef shin is cut into pieces and set on a plate together with the boned pieces of calves' foot. The remaining juice and chick-peas are put together in a gravy bowl. The dates are not eaten, they colour the dish without sweetening it. If the cooking of *dafina* has been successful, the meat must be caramelised, the potatoes brown, very soft and almost candied, the wheat grains look like gold nuggets, the eggs have a beautiful beige colour and the chick-pea stock is creamy and brown.

chick-pea purée

Traditional recipe:

SERVES 4 AS A SIDE DISH

500 g (1 lb 2 oz) chick-peas

1 clove

1 onion, peeled

6 parsley sprigs

2 thyme sprigs

1 celery stick

1 bay leaf

2 garlic cloves, peeled

1 teaspoon salt

150 g (5$^{1}/_{2}$ oz) butter

250 ml (9 fl oz) single cream

$^{1}/_{2}$ teaspoon salt

$^{1}/_{2}$ teaspoon ground white pepper

1 tablespoon olive oil

1 tablespoon chopped fresh
flat-leaved parsley

$^{1}/_{4}$ teaspoon grated nutmeg

The day before, soak the chick-peas in a large quantity of cold water. The next day, drain and rinse the chick-peas. Stick the clove in the onion. Attach together the parsley, the thyme, the celery stick and the bay leaf in a *bouquet garni*. In a pan, put the chick-peas, add the onion, whole, the *bouquet garni*, the garlic cloves and the salt and cover with water. Bring to the boil and cook, uncovered, for 1$^{1}/_{4}$ hours on medium heat. If necessary, add water during the cooking.

Drain the chick-peas, discard the onion, and *bouquet garni* and mash the chick-peas together with the garlic in a food processor.

In a pan, melt the butter, add the cream and bring to the boil. Off the heat, add the chick-pea purée, and the $^{1}/_{2}$ teaspoon each of salt and pepper. Stir thoroughly with a wooden spoon. Put the purée in a serving dish. Dig a little hole in the centre and pour in the olive oil and the chopped parsley. Sprinkle nutmeg on the purée and serve hot.

roasted prawns with cumin
served on a carrot and orange salad

This recipe is shown on page 167.

Modern recipe:

SERVES 4 AS A MAIN DISH

750 g (1 lb 10 oz) carrots

5 juicy and seedless oranges

4 garlic cloves

juice of 1 lime

1/2 teaspoon salt

1/2 teaspoon ground white pepper

1/2 teaspoon cornflour

2 tablespoons water

1 tablespoon chopped fresh coriander, to garnish

For the prawns:

12 large or 16 medium-size raw king prawns

1 teaspoon ground cumin

3 tablespoons olive oil

salt and pepper

The day before, peel 500 g (1 lb 2 oz) of the carrots and cut them into *julienne* strips. With a zester, remove long strips of orange zest from two oranges. Blanch the orange strips by putting them in boiling water for less than a minute and then immediately plunging them into iced water. Repeat this operation three times.

Put the orange and carrot strips in a bowl and add the whole garlic cloves. Cover the bowl with cling film and refrigerate for 24 hours.

The next day, remove and discard the heads and the shells from the prawns, cut them in half lengthways and de-vein them. Put them in a bowl covered with cling film and refrigerate.

Peel the remaining carrots and then squeeze them in a juice extractor. Squeeze the juice of the three remaining oranges. Mix together the carrot juice, the orange juice and the lime juice. Season to taste with the salt and pepper, transfer to a saucepan and bring to the boil.

Mix the cornflour with the 2 tablespoons of cold water. Off the heat, add the cornflour mixture to the carrot, orange and lime juice and stir in well. Leave to cool for 2 hours.

Remove completely the pith of the two oranges that were used for the zest and cut their flesh into 1 cm (1/2-inch) cubes.

Take the bowl of carrot and orange-zest strips out of the fridge. Remove the garlic cloves. Add the diced oranges and mix everything together. Divide the mixture between the centres of four serving plates and sprinkle with the fresh coriander. Then pour the creamy carrot, lime and orange juice around the salad and let it soak the salad while you cook the prawns.

Sprinkle a little salt and pepper and all the cumin over the prawns. Put a frying-pan over a fairly high heat, add the olive oil and, when hot, fry the prawns for 2 minutes, stirring to colour them evenly. Top each plate of salad with three or four prawns and serve immediately.

sea bass fillet
served on a warm tabbouleh
with citrus fruit juice

Modern recipe;

SERVES 4 AS A MAIN COURSE

4 sea bass fillets

1 teaspoon salt

1/2 teaspoon ground white pepper

4 oranges

2 lemons

250 g (9 oz) couscous

200 ml (7 fl oz) olive oil

1 red pepper, de-seeded and chopped finely

1 green pepper, de-seeded and chopped finely

Season the sea bass fillets with a little salt and pepper and keep aside in a colander. Remove the zest from two of the oranges and one of the lemons with a sharp knife or zester and cut them in small pieces. Blanch the orange and lemon zests by putting them in boiling water for 30 seconds and then immediately plunging them into iced water. Repeat this operation three times. Drain and keep aside.

Steam the couscous as explained on page 115.

Heat a tablespoon of the olive oil in a saucepan on medium to high heat and fry the peppers, stirring, for 2 minutes; they should stay quite crisp. Off the heat, add the couscous and citrus zests to the peppers and season with salt and pepper. Mix everything and cover to keep warm.

Squeeze the juices from all the oranges and lemons, adding half the pulp without the pips to the juice. Then bring the juice to the boil in a small saucepan. Keep aside 2 tablespoonfuls of the oil and add the rest to the fruit juice while stirring. Season with salt and pepper to taste.

Heat the remaining oil in a non-stick frying-pan and add the sea bass fillets. Fry them for 2 minutes on each side.

Then put the *tabbouleh* in the middle of four warm serving plates, put a sea bass fillet on the top and serve with the citrus sauce around.

Clockwise from top left: couscous; fishing boats at Essaouira; Roasted Prawns with Cumin served on a Carrot and Orange Salad (page 165); Sea Bass Fillet served on a Warm Tabbouleh with Citrus Fruit Juice

couscous with fish Momo's way

Modern recipe:

SERVES 4

For the couscous:

500 g (1 lb 2 oz) medium-grain couscous

800 ml (1 pint 7 fl oz) water

1 teaspoon salt

100 ml (3½ fl oz) olive oil

4 tablespoons finely chopped
fresh coriander

4 tablespoons finely chopped
fresh flat-leaved parsley

For the fish:

4 fillets of red snapper, bones reserved

4 fillets of sea bass, bones reserved

½ teaspoon salt

½ teaspoon ground white pepper

For the stock:

200 ml (7 fl oz) olive oil

2 onions, chopped

250 g (9 oz) carrots, peeled and
cut into large cubes

2 tomatoes, peeled, de-seeded
and coarsely chopped

1 fennel bulb, chopped

1 celery stick, chopped

1 teaspoon aniseeds

1 soup spoon concentrated tomato purée

2 whole garlic cloves, peeled

1 clove

1 teaspoon salt

½ teaspoon ground white pepper

In the stock-pot of the *couscoussier* (lower part), heat the olive oil, add the fish bones and onions. Cook for 5 minutes and then add the carrots, tomatoes, fennel, celery, aniseeds, tomato purée, garlic and clove. Season with salt and pepper. Pour in water to cover and bring to the boil. Lower the heat, fit the upper part (steamer) in order to steam the couscous as explained on page 115. Cook for 2 hours on a low heat. Gently remove the fish bones after 35 minutes.

Sprinkle salt and pepper on the fish fillets. Ten minutes before the end of cooking, put the fish fillets in the upper part of the *couscoussier* (steamer) and cook them in the steam from the stock.

After the last steaming of the couscous, add the olive oil, add the chopped coriander and parsley and mix thoroughly.

On warmed serving plates, put a layer of hot couscous and top with 1 fillet of each fish. The strained stock can be served separately, in a soup tureen.

couscous
with seven vegetables

Traditional recipe:

SERVES 8

For the stock:

1 small white cabbage, quartered

1 kg (2¼ lb) knuckle of veal or shoulder of lamb, cut into large chunks

2 large onions, quartered

500 g (1 lb 2 oz) carrots, peeled and cut into 3 cm (1½-inch) pieces

250 g (9 oz) small turnips, peeled and quartered

2 peppers, de-seeded and cut into large strips

8 coriander sprigs, tied with string

1 teaspoon *ras-el-hanout* (see page 36) or 100 ml (3½ fl oz) prepared saffron (see page 68)

50 g (1¾ oz) unsalted butter

1 teaspoon salt

1 teaspoon ground white pepper

5 unpeeled tomatoes, quartered

2 aubergines, peeled and cut into chunks

500 g (1 lb 2 oz) courgettes, halved lengthways and then cut into 3 cm (1½-inch) pieces

For the couscous:

1 kg (2¼ lb) medium-grade couscous

800 ml (1 pint 7 fl oz) water

1 teaspoon salt

80 g (3 oz) unsalted butter, cut into pieces

For serving:

1 tablespoon harissa (see page 148)

1 garlic clove, crushed

1 teaspoon ground cumin

½ teaspoon salt and 1 tablespoon olive oil, to season the *harissa* if necessary

Blanch the cabbage by putting it in boiling water for 30 seconds and then immediately plunging it into iced water. Repeat this operation three times. Drain and keep aside.

In the lower part (stock-pot) of a *couscoussier* (see page 219), put the pieces of meat, add the onions, carrots, turnips, peppers, coriander sprigs, *ras-el-hanout* or prepared saffron, butter, salt and pepper. Cover with water. Bring to the boil, lower the heat and fit the upper part (steamer) in order to steam the couscous as explained on page 115. Leave the meat and vegetables to cook in the stock for 30 minutes, while steaming the couscous above the stock.

After 30 minutes, add the cabbage, tomatoes, aubergines and courgettes and leave to cook for 30 more minutes. Check that the meat is cooked and remove it to prevent from disintegrating if the couscous steaming is not finished. In that case, don't forget to re-heat the meat in the stock before serving.

Add the garlic, cumin, salt and olive oil to the *harissa* (if not seasoned before), mix everything and put in a small dish.

Put the couscous in a large, warmed serving dish in a mound with a well in the middle. Put the meat in the centre and arrange the vegetables around the meat. Remove the onions and coriander from the stock, serve it separately in a soup tureen and also serve the *harissa* separately.

dried fruit salad
with aromatic spices

Modern recipe:

SERVES 5

100 g (3½ oz) stoned prunes

100 g (3½ oz) dried apricots

100 g (3½ oz) dried figs

90 g (3 oz) blanched almonds
(see page 135)

90 g (3 oz) walnut halves

50 g (2 oz) sesame seeds, toasted,
to decorate

For the syrup:

1 litre (1¾ pints) water

150 ml (¼ pint) orange-blossom water

150 g (5½ oz) brown granulated sugar

5 cloves

2 cinnamon sticks

½ teaspoon grated nutmeg

juice of 2 limes

To make the syrup, bring the water to the boil and add the orange-blossom water and sugar. Reduce the heat to very low and add the cloves, cinnamon sticks and grated nutmeg. Cook gently for one hour. Leave the syrup to cool and then add the lime juice and stir.

Toast the almonds in a dry frying-pan.

Put the three dried fruits in a large bowl and pour the syrup and spices on top. Cover with cling film and leave the fruits to macerate in the mixture overnight in the fridge, in order to give the syrup's aromas to the fruits.

One hour before serving, add the walnuts and almonds.

Remove the cinnamon sticks and the cloves. Serve the fruits in the syrup after having sprinkled the fruit salad with toasted sesame seeds, just before serving.

PASTRIES AND SWEETS

All North Africans love pastries: delicate, sugary pastries, flavoured with the most fragrant of orange-blossom water; pastries dripping with honey; or elaborately coiled pastries that are served with heavily sugared mint tea.

All of this is enough to send most of us into a diabetic shock, but it is an integral part of their culture. Every neighbourhood in Tunisia has its own pâtisserie and each shop will have dozens of varieties of sweets. Buying pâtisserie appears to be almost more fun than eating it. During *ramadan*, I went from one Tunisian pastry shop to another and was stunned to see crowds of people buying overstuffed boxes of sweets, which they would eat after they broke their fast. The anguish on their faces over whether or not to choose the heavy slices of gâteau or the honeyed biscuits was unforgettable, as was the sense of anticipation of that first bite.

Glace (ice cream) is as popular as *gelato* is in Italy and can be made with fresh fruit, almonds or coffee. The most popular Tunisian ice cream is the *sabayon*, made with egg yolks. It is served in all the Tunisian restaurants in the Faubourg Montmartre and in Belleville in Paris. *Sabayon* is served for dessert, together with a vast selection of fresh fruits, peeled and beautifully set on a large tray with ice cubes: watermelon, cherries, grapes, strawberries, apricots, melon and plums in a superb palette of colours. Here are some favourite North African pastries.

Gazelle horns Delicate, horn-shaped pastries filled with almond paste and sugar.

Zlabiya A snake-like pastry with a crisp shell. Dark brown in colour, with honey drizzled over it.

Makroude Light brown, made with wheat and semolina and stuffed with dates and honey.

Laghribria A tall, almond-sugar creation.

Kalbelouz Literally 'heart of the almond'. Made with semolina and almonds.

Dattes fourrées Tunisians love dates and these – stuffed with lightly coloured almond paste – are devoured with glee.

Droo A cake made of sorghum (a corn-like grain).

A plate of North African pastries: gazelle horns and *riba*

croustillants of roasted figs
with almonds and cinnamon

Modern recipe:

SERVES 6

For the custard:

500 ml (18 fl oz) milk

1 vanilla pod

6 egg yolks

90 g (3 oz) caster sugar

For the croustillants:

150 g (5^1/$_2$ oz) butter

150 g (5^1/$_2$ oz) brown sugar

400 g (14 oz) fresh ripe unpeeled black figs, chopped

250 g (9 oz) blanched almonds (see page 135), toasted and chopped

1^1/$_2$ teaspoons ground cinnamon

6 *ouarka* sheets (see page 70)

1 tablespoon icing sugar

Preheat the oven to 170°C/320°F/Gas Mark 3.

To make the custard, bring the milk to the boil, with the vanilla pod. Meanwhile, beat the egg yolks with the sugar for 2–3 minutes until pale and thick. When the milk boils, pour it slowly over the egg and sugar while stirring. Then transfer the mixture to the pan and whisk well, over a gentle heat, until the sauce begins to thicken. Then remove from the heat, leave to cool and refrigerate until cold.

To make the *croustillants*, melt 100 g (3^1/$_2$ oz) of the butter in a frying-pan, then add the sugar and stir in order to start a caramel. When the caramel is golden, add the figs, almonds and 1 teaspoon of the cinnamon, mix well and cook for 2–3 minutes. Set aside to cool.

Cut each *ouarka* sheet in four equal, triangular pieces. Put a tablespoon of the filling in the centre of each triangle. Pull up the angles of the triangle and tie them in the shape of a purse, holding them together with a cocktail stick. Brush the little parcels with the remaining melted butter and arrange on a greased baking sheet. Bake for 3–4 minutes until crisp and golden. Remove the cocktail sticks carefully and sprinkle a little icing sugar and a pinch of the remaining ground cinnamon on each fig and almond parcel. Put four small *croustillants* on each serving dish. Surround with the custard, after having removed the vanilla pod.

montecaos

Traditional recipe:

SERVES 4

100 g (3½ oz) wheat flour
1 teaspoon baking powder
pinch of salt
50 g (1¾ oz) icing sugar
125 g (4½ oz) melted butter
ground cinnamon, to decorate

Preheat the oven to 150°C/300°F/Gas Mark 2.

In a bowl, mix the flour, baking powder, salt and sugar. Add the melted butter and mix thoroughly with your hands while pressing the dough, until you get a homogenous paste. Lightly sprinkle a baking tray with flour. Take little pieces of the dough, the size of a walnut, roll them in the shape of a ball and then flatten them slightly. Set them on the baking tray as you make them, leaving a space of 2 cm (¾ inch) between each *montecao*. Sprinkle a pinch of cinnamon on each *montecao* and bake for 15 to 20 minutes. When cooked, the *montecaos* are slightly cracked on the top and should not be coloured.

Couple resting after harvesting olives in Tunisia

beghrir   spongy pancakes with honey

Traditional recipe:

SERVES 6

40 g (1½ oz) fresh yeast
300 ml (½ pint) warm water
1 sugar cube
375 g (13 oz) wheat flour
125 g (4½ oz) semolina
½ teaspoon salt
3 eggs
250 ml (9 fl oz) warm milk
250 ml (9 fl oz) warm water
100 ml (3½ fl oz) sunflower oil

To serve:

300 g (10½ oz) blanched almonds
(see page 135)
150 g (5½ oz) honey

In a bowl, dissolve the yeast with the 300 ml (½ pint) of warm water and sugar cube and leave it to activate for 20 minutes.

Sieve the flour and semolina and mix them with the salt in a large bowl. Add the eggs in the middle and mix with your hand, forming circles until the dough is homogeneous. Then add the yeast and pour the milk and the water, little by little, while continuing to mix thoroughly. Cover the bowl with a clean cloth and leave to stand for 1–2 hours, at room temperature, until the dough is fluffy and the volume has doubled.

Toast the blanched almonds in a dry frying-pan by stirring constantly with a wooden spoon until golden. Leave them to cool out of the pan and then grind them coarsely.

Before starting to cook the *beghrir*, spread a damp clean cloth on a table.

Brush a heavy-based, non-stick frying-pan with some of the oil and heat it on medium heat. Then, using a small ladle, stir the dough and pour some of it in the pan in the shape of a 12 cm (5-inch) diameter, 3 mm (⅛ inch) thick pancake and cook only on one side until the bottom side gets a light golden colour. The pancake is cooked when the surface forms plenty of little holes. Set the pancake on the damp cloth to keep it moist. Continue cooking the pancakes until the dough is finished. The pancakes shouldn't be stacked while still hot.

Serve the *beghrir*, warm or cold, with almonds and/or honey.

When left over, *beghrir* can be heated quickly on both sides, in a pan with a little butter.

Beghrir is a North African spongy pancake, traditionally served with mint tea (see page 144), for breakfast or in the afternoon. Smooth on the bottom side and sprinkled with dozens of little holes on the top side, it is served with a choice of sugar, honey or butter and almonds. *Beghrir* is one of many kinds of North African pancakes that include a sweet version of *rghaif* (see Seafood *Rghaif*, page 74), *msemna* and *mofleta* which is a very thin pancake, traditionally cooked on a metal round cover over a *kanoun* (brazier). *Mofleta* is a Moroccan Jewish speciality served at *Mimouna* (see *Jabane*, page 133). And above all the famous *sfenj*, a fluffy doughnut, made fresh several times a day, and deep-fried in a huge basin full of oil, removed with a special long hook and sold like a necklace made with a long palm-heart leaf. *Sfenj* are traditionally served with caster sugar or liquid honey. One can find them in any Moroccan town.

Clockwise from top left: North African honey; deep-frying *sfenj* (doughnuts); *Beghrir*; two *sfenj* makers

makroude with dates

Traditional recipe:

MAKES 30 TO 35 MAKROUDE

For the makroude:

350 g (12 oz) thin semolina

150 g (5^1/$_2$ oz) wheat flour

1 tablespoon baking powder

^{1}/$_2$ teaspoon salt

3 small eggs

125 g (4^1/$_2$ oz) caster sugar

400 ml (14 fl oz) sunflower oil

100 ml (3^1/$_2$ fl oz) water

For the date paste:

250 g (9 oz) soft dates, stoned

grated zest of ^{1}/$_2$ orange

^{1}/$_2$ teaspoon ground cinnamon

^{1}/$_4$ teaspoon ground ginger

^{1}/$_4$ teaspoon ground cloves

2 tablespoons sunflower oil

For the syrup:

250 g (9 oz) caster sugar

1 tablespoon clear honey

150 ml (^{1}/$_4$ pint) water

juice of 1 lemon

1 tablespoon orange-blossom water

First prepare the *makroude* paste. Heat a dry, heavy-based frying-pan. Add the semolina and toast it on very low heat while stirring constantly with a wooden spoon until the semolina is completely dried and gets a light golden colour. Pour the semolina into a bowl and leave to cool. Then add the flour, the baking powder, and salt. Mix thoroughly and keep the mixture aside.

Separate the eggs, yolks in one bowl and whites in another bowl. Add the sugar to the egg yolks and whisk for 2–3 minutes until pale and slightly thick. Then add 100 ml (3^1/$_2$ fl oz) of the oil and the water and mix thoroughly with a wooden spoon.

Whisk the egg whites until they are very thick. Fold them gently into the egg yolks and mix thoroughly. Pour the semolina and flour mixture slowly into the eggs and mix with your hand until you get a thick paste. Keep aside.

Then prepare the date paste. Mince the dates with a meat mincer or a food processor. Add the orange zest to the date paste. Then add the cinnamon, ginger, cloves and oil. Mix and squeeze all the ingredients together with your hands, to form a soft, homogenous paste. Oil your hands and shape the date paste into a long cylinder 2 cm (^{3}/$_4$ inch) thick. Keep aside on an oiled plate.

Shape the *makroude* paste into a long cylinder 4 cm (1^3/$_4$ inches) thick, then spread it on a slightly floured surface with a rolling pin until the cylinder becomes 9 cm (3^1/$_2$ inches) wide.

Flatten the date paste cylinder with your fingers until it becomes 4 cm (1³/₄ inches) wide. Put the date paste in the centre of the *makroude*, leaving 2 cm (³/₄ inch) on one side and 3 cm (1¹/₂ inches) on the other side. Then cover the date paste with the *makroude* paste in order to form a flat roll that should be about 5 cm (2 inches) wide. Smooth the top of the paste with your fingers in order to seal the two edges together and to rub them out. Cut the *makroude* roll in pieces of 3 cm (1¹/₂ inches) long, diagonally. Each section of the *makroude* should clearly show the dark brown date filling surrounded with the golden semolina paste.

Heat the oil for deep-frying. Add the *makroudes* and fry them until they are lightly browned all over. Scoop out with a slotted spoon and drain on kitchen paper to remove any excess oil.

To prepare the syrup: put the sugar, honey and water in a heavy-based pan on medium heat and stir with a wooden spoon until the sugar has melted; then lower the heat and leave to simmer for 10 minutes. Add the lemon juice, stir and leave to cook on very low heat for 10 more minutes. Off the heat add the orange-blossom water and mix with the syrup. For the *makroudes*, the syrup must not colour and not be too thick.

Dip the *makroudes* in the warm syrup and scoop them out with a slotted spoon. Put on a serving dish. Serve warm or cold.

Above: dates; below: harvesting dates

Everything, in this Algeria, had been a revelation for him, a source of distress even – of anguish. A sky too serene, a sun too dazzling, an atmosphere in which they languished, like a slow sigh that invited indolence and idle voluptuousness, the solemnity of a people draped in white, whose soul he could not penetrate, the deep green vegetation, contrasting with the rocky grey or red soil, parched and apparently desiccated, and then something indefinable, but bewildering and intoxicating, which emanated from an unknown source, all this had agitated him, had caused to burst forth in him wellsprings of emotion of which he had never suspected the existence.

Isabelle Eberhardt, *Au Pays Des Sables*

Algeria

ARRIVAL IN ALGERIA

I arrived in Algiers at night, flying from Barcelona. It was the height of summer and the aeroplane was packed. I was the only non-Algerian on board and there was a sense of high anticipation throughout the short journey, which was punctuated by drastic pitches of the plane: we were in the midst of a violent rainstorm. It appeared to be an omen.

Most of the men and women on board were returning home from their summer holidays. They were loud, boisterous and energetic. I was nervous because I was going somewhere that I had never been before and to a place that held a strong fascination for me, a vivid and alluring picture in my mind. But it was not an easy place to reach: it had taken me six months to obtain a visa to enter Algeria. The day I left, the Berber protest singer Matoub Lounes was assassinated in Kabylie and the government stopped all journalists from entering the country. I made it into the country with a whisper of luck.

The airport of Algiers was exactly what I expected: sultry, smoky and seedy; retro, like something out of another time and place. It looked like a film set from a 1950s Humphrey Bogart movie. There was the smell of jasmine in the air. I could see the families reuniting, kissing and hugging and I heard women making the sound of the *youyous*, the cry of celebration. A row of soldiers was waiting in front of passport control and a group of heavy-looking bodyguards. As soon as I had my passport stamped they approached me as three of them were mine, assigned by the government for my protection during the two weeks that I would be in the country.

We drove into town along the darkened sea and then to my hotel, an old converted palace called the Al Djezair, where Eisenhower stayed during the desert campaign of World War II.

My room had French doors which opened onto a vast, magical rose garden. By the light of the nearly full moon, I walked through endless rows of flowers. Somewhere in the distance, I could hear people laughing and seductive haunting music: horns, cymbals and drums. A Berber boy brought me a tray with the deepest, sweetest mint tea and a plate of Algerian sweet biscuits.

> It is the man who makes money, but it is the woman who builds the house.
>
> Arabic proverb

ALGERIA

Algeria is seductive and bewitching. It has inspired countless artists, writers and musicians with its incredible beauty and its intense light.

Algeria is not as well known as the other Maghreb countries. It has never fostered tourism like its neighbours. While Morocco and Tunisia each receive more than 3.5 million tourists annually, Algeria maybe achieves 20 per cent of that and in recent times probably even less because of the civil strife. It has an area of more than 900,000 square miles – five times the size of France – but 85 per cent is Saharan desert. Most of the population is concentrated along the coast (Algeria has beautiful beaches).

Algeria was the first North African country to be conquered by France and the last to gain independence. The Maghreb used to be compared to a bird: Algeria was the main body and Morocco and Tunisia the wings. It was said that the bird would not fly until the body was free. Algeria has been going through a tumultuous transition. It is still in that process and will hopefully soon gain its freedom to fly.

Ruined medieval village near Kabylie

THE FOOD OF ALGERIA

Oddly enough, Algerian cuisine is often disregarded. 'There is no such thing as Algerian cuisine', is a phrase I have heard more often than I would care to think about. It is simply not true: how could the third largest country in Africa not have a cuisine? Algerian cuisine is very rich and varies greatly from the east to the west. In the west it is influenced by Morocco and has many sweet recipes. In the east, it resembles the cuisine of Tunisia with red sauces and honeyed pastries. In the countryside and the mountains traditional, very simple dishes are still cooked.

Algerian food draws on the influences of the country's conquerors: the Turks who left behind some of their classic dishes, such as *dolmas*, stuffed vegetables, and *bourek* (which is a pastry-like roll filled with meat or other kinds of fillings). Cereal is important to the Algerian diet. Wheat or *frik* is used in couscous and in numerous *chorbas* (a type of soup). Many Algerian recipes are well known across the North African region. *Mechoui* (roasted lamb) and couscous occupy a prominent place in the cuisine. In the south hot mint tea is drunk all day long to quench the thirst.

You have bread and I have bread, so why envy?

Arabic proverb

Algeria borders the Mediterranean and so there is the opportunity to eat good fish. The El Djenina restaurant near the old *kasbah* in Algiers is run by an elegant Madame who oversees the small restaurant with a sharp eye; there one can eat whole fish grilled in spices, or squid, prawns and octopus. All of these fish are very popular in Algeria. Sardines are cooked by most families, in incredibly imaginative ways: rolled into balls, made into patties, spiced, stuffed or served in a salad.

Other classic dishes include *chorba* (soups made with cereals and sometimes meat) followed by a *kesksou bil djedj*, a chicken couscous which is the staple of the Algerian diet and is served for every party, circumcision, funeral or wedding.

Couscous Just as in the other countries of the Maghreb, couscous varies from region to region and may be cooked with meat, fish, chicken or honey, and with white or red sauces. The type of grain also varies. Setif, a famous granary in North Africa, produces a very fine couscous grain, while western Algeria's couscous is coarser. Couscous is usually made from scratch by women early in the morning, sifting the semolina or barley, through their fingers in a large metal bowl, usually placed on the floor. Couscous can also be sweet – such as couscous with dates, or a couscous recipe I found in an ancient cookbook in Algiers, the central ingredient of which was milk. One incredibly popular dish is a couscous from the Kabylie region, which is made with carrots, courgettes, dried onions, lamb and tomatoes. Another couscous with seven vegetables (*kesksou b'l khodra*), is served throughout Algeria. The coastal cities have their own version of fish couscous, using cod, scrod or snapper – basically any fish that will not fall apart when cooked and which is full of flavour. It is then served in a red sauce that is made from tomatoes and *harissa*. In Oran couscous can be made with shellfish.

Feast days and celebrations Feast days and celebrations are important to Algerians. When a child is born, a party may go on for as long as a week. In Kabylie, the mountainous region inhabited by a fair-skinned Berber tribe, extended families live together in villages in the same manner that they have lived for centuries. The arrival of a new baby, the return of a relative from a long sojourn in France, or a marriage can set off a celebration that can last for nearly a week – or sometimes longer. Long tables are laid out, food is brought, dancing and music begin and families reunite. In western Algeria where potatoes are a favoured food, enormous *tagines*, such as *tagine au chou-fleur* (*tagine* with cauliflower fritters served on a bed of French-fried potatoes) might be served, or a *tagine* of lamb, olives and mushrooms.

MUSIC OF ALGERIA

The music, just like the architecture or the folklore, has been influenced and enriched by Algeria's different occupiers. Oran is the birthplace of Rai music, that sensual blend of Oriental and Western music. In Kabylie, the protest singer Matoub Lounes wrote haunting and provocative lyrics. Khaled, perhaps the most well known Algerian singer, has influenced many major European artists. Algerian rap music, which was born on the streets of Algiers, is an expression of the frustration and complexities of the young people who constitute the majority of the population.

couscous salad in tabbouleh style

Traditional recipe:

SERVES 5 AS A STARTER OR SALAD

500 g (1 lb 2 oz) couscous

$^1/_2$ cucumber, de-seeded and chopped

3 large tomatoes, skinned,
de-seeded and chopped

$^1/_2$ green pepper, de-seeded
and chopped

6 spring onions, chopped

$^1/_2$ celery stick, chopped

3 tablespoons chopped fresh mint

3 tablespoons chopped fresh coriander

3 tablespoons chopped fresh
flat-leaved parsley

juice of 2 lemons

5 tablespoons olive oil

1 teaspoon salt

$^1/_2$ teaspoon ground white pepper

Prepare and cook the couscous as described on page 115. Leave to cool.

Put the chopped cucumber in a colander, sprinkle with salt and leave to drain for 30 minutes.

Rinse and pat dry carefully. Mix all the ingredients together carefully. Refrigerate and serve cold.

chorba frik
crushed wheat soup

Traditional recipe:

SERVES 4

300 g (10½ oz) boneless lamb

150 ml (¼ pint) olive oil

1 large onion, finely chopped

6 tablespoons finely chopped
fresh coriander

1.5 litres (2¾ pints) water

1 teaspoon salt

½ teaspoon ground white pepper

1 teaspoon paprika

1 teaspoon dried mint

150 g (5½ oz) crushed wheat (*frik*)

1 teaspoon concentrated tomato purée

2 lemons, quartered, to serve

Slice the meat in very small and thin slices. Heat the oil in a large saucepan and fry the onion together with the meat. When golden, add half the coriander and pour in the water. Add the salt, pepper, paprika, dried mint, and crushed wheat (*frik*). Dilute the tomato purée in 2 tablespoons of water and add it. Stir and leave to cook, covered, on a low heat, for about 50 minutes.

Add the remaining coriander just before serving. Check the seasoning and serve hot, with lemon quarters.

potaje beef soup with beans and pumpkin

Traditional recipe:

SERVES 6

350 g (12 oz) dried beans
500 g (1 lb 2 oz) shin of beef
2 marrow-bones
1 teaspoon salt
1 teaspoon ground white pepper
3 litres (5¼ pints) water
750 g (1 lb 10 oz) swiss chard
1 sweet potato
250 g (9 oz) pumpkin
12 garlic cloves, peeled
1 tablespoon paprika
1 tablespoon ground cumin
juice of 1 lemon
100 ml (3½ fl oz) sunflower oil

The day before, soak the dried beans in cold water.

The next day, in a stockpot or large pan, put the meat, the bones, the beans and the salt and pepper. Add the water. Bring to the boil and cover. Then put the heat to medium and leave to cook for 1½ hours. If necessary, use a slotted spoon to skim with a slotted spoon off any froth that may rise to the surface because of the meat and marrow-bones.

Remove the marrow-bones after 1 hour and keep them aside on a plate. Check the meat after 1 hour to see if tender and remove it from the stock when cooked, to prevent it from disintegrating. If not, leave to cook for 30 more minutes.

When cooked, remove the meat and keep aside, covered with foil. The meat and the bones are added later to the soup to heat through before serving.

Cut the swiss chards and use just the green parts in the *potaje*. The white parts can be kept for another recipe. Wash and chop very coarsely the green parts. Peel the sweet potato and dice it. Peel the pumpkin and clean it of any seeds or strands that it may contain. Cut it in large cubes.

Add the swiss chards, pumpkin and sweet potato to the stockpot. Leave to cook, covered, on medium heat for 1 hour.

When the beans are soft, smash them roughly, as well as the pumpkin and sweet potato, with a wooden spoon against the edges of the pan. Add the garlic, paprika, cumin, lemon juice and oil. Uncover the pan and simmer on medium to high heat until the garlic is soft. Add the meats and bones to re-heat 5 minutes before serving. Check the seasoning and serve very hot with one or two entire garlic cloves and a piece of meat on each plate.

roasted red mullet
served with chokada sauce

The roasted red mullet served with *chokada* sauce is an excellent summer dish, typical of Algeria. It combines a slightly marinated grilled fish with a very tasty dip: the *chokada* sauce. *Chokada* sauce may also be served with steamed vegetables (cauliflower, broccoli, potatoes), as a starter, or, as an appetiser, with sticks of raw vegetables (carrots, cucumber, celery), or even with hard-boiled eggs, instead of a mayonnaise.

Traditional recipe:

SERVES 4 AS A MAIN COURSE

For the chokada sauce:
8 anchovies, preserved in olive oil
50 ml (2 fl oz) olive oil
1 tablespoon wheat flour
50 ml (2 fl oz) water
1/2 teaspoon freshly ground black pepper
juice of 1 lemon
1 egg yolk

For the fish:
100 ml (3 1/2 fl oz) olive oil
1 fennel heart
juice of 1 lemon
1 teaspoon salt
1 teaspoon ground white pepper
16 small red mullet

Prepare the *chokada* sauce first. Chop the anchovies finely and fry them in olive oil, on low heat. Sprinkle with the flour and stir with a wooden spoon to mix with the anchovies. Add the water and continue stirring in order to get a smooth sauce. Then add the pepper, the lemon juice and the egg yolk and continue stirring on the lowest possible heat in order to thicken the sauce. Put the sauce in a bowl and leave it to cool.

Prepare a marinade with half the olive oil, the fennel heart, lemon juice, salt and pepper.

Scale the red mullets without gutting them. Rinse quickly under running water and dry them with kitchen paper. Put the red mullets in the marinade and leave for 1 hour.

Brush the grill with olive oil, heat it and grill the red mullets on both sides for 3–4 minutes on each side. Serve hot, together with the *chokada* sauce.

lhem lahlou *sweet lamb stew*

Traditional recipe:

SERVES 4 AS A MAIN COURSE

32 prunes

50 g (1³/4 oz) toasted sesame seeds

100 g (3¹/2 oz) unsalted butter

1 kg (2¹/4 lb) lean boneless lamb, cut into chunks

1 teaspoon salt

¹/2 teaspoon ground white pepper

1 teaspoon ground cinnamon

2 cinnamon sticks

150 g (5¹/2 oz) brown caster sugar

100 ml (3¹/2 fl oz) orange-blossom water

300 ml (¹/2 pint) water

2 apples

In the upper part of a steamer, steam the prunes for 30 minutes until swollen. Leave to cool and remove the stone. Toast the sesame seeds in dry frying-pan, stirring constantly until golden. Leave to cool. Roll the prunes in the toasted sesame seeds.

Melt the butter in a large *tagine* plate or a flameproof casserole dish, add the meat, salt and pepper and fry on medium heat, stirring, for about 10 minutes until the meat pieces are an even light brown. Sprinkle on the ground cinnamon and add the cinnamon sticks. Add the sugar little by little. Then add the orange-blossom water and pour on the water to cover. Bring to the boil, then reduce the heat and simmer for 20 minutes.

Peel, core and thinly slice the apples and add them to the dish, with the prunes. Cook for another 20 minutes, uncovered, on low to medium heat, to allow the water to evaporate. Check the seasoning and serve hot. This dish is delicious served with Potato Gratin with Fresh Coriander (see page 100) or Fennel and Courgette Compote with Aniseed (see page 98).

kefta with eggs

Traditional recipe:

SERVES 4 AS A MAIN COURSE

For the kefta:

450 g (1 lb) boneless beef or
lamb, minced

50 g (1³/₄ oz) beef or lamb fat, minced

3 tablespoons chopped fresh coriander

3 tablespoons chopped fresh
flat-leaved parsley

1 onion, finely grated

1 teaspoon ground cumin

1¹/₂ teaspoons paprika

¹/₄ teaspoon Cayenne pepper

¹/₄ teaspoon ground white pepper

1 small teaspoon salt

1 tablespoon sunflower oil

2 tablespoons water

For the eggs:

75 g (2³/₄ oz) unsalted butter

4 eggs

¹/₂ teaspoon paprika

pinch of Cayenne pepper

¹/₄ teaspoon salt

To make the *kefta*, put the minced meat and minced fat in a large bowl. Add all the ingredients and knead everything together with your hands, for 5 minutes, until perfectly mixed.

Put some oil in a little bowl and oil your hands slightly, then take a small quantity of the *kefta* mixture and shape it with your hands, to the shape and size of a large marble. Continue in the same manner until the *kefta* mixture is finished. Put the keftas on an oiled tray as you shape them.

Heat the butter in a large *tagine* plate or flameproof casserole dish and brown the meatballs, turning them regularly to colour them all over. The *keftas* will give off quite a bit of juice. Remove the *keftas* from the dish and keep aside. Raise the heat to reduce and thicken the juice. Return the *kefta* to the *tagine*. Break the eggs carefully on the *kefta* and sprinkle with the paprika, Cayenne pepper and salt. Cook until the egg whites are just set and the yolk is still soft and serve at once, while still very hot.

chicken liver m'chermel

chicken liver in piquant sauce

Traditional recipe:

SERVES 5 AS A MAIN COURSE

6 tablespoons chopped fresh coriander

6 tablespoons chopped fresh
flat-leaved parsley

1 teaspoon ground cumin

1 teaspoon paprika

1/4 teaspoon Cayenne pepper

juice of 2 lemons

1 teaspoon salt

1/2 teaspoon ground white pepper

1 kg (2 1/4 lb) chicken livers,
trimmed and halved

5 tablespoons wheat flour

100 ml (3 1/2 fl oz) sunflower oil

2 mild fresh chillies, de-seeded
and cut into rings

500 g (1 lb 2 oz) tomatoes, skinned,
de-seeded and chopped

100 g (3 1/2 oz) green olives, stoned

1 pickled lemon (see page 141)

Mix together the coriander, parsley, cumin, paprika, Cayenne pepper and lemon juice. Season with half the salt and pepper and marinate the chicken livers in this mixture for 45 minutes.

Mix the flour with the remaining salt and pepper and coat the livers in the seasoned flour. Heat the oil in a large frying-pan and fry the livers quickly, on high heat, for 2 minutes, stirring, until golden. Remove from the pan and set aside on a plate. Add the chillies and the tomatoes to the pan and leave the mixture to cook on high heat for 5 minutes, while stirring.

Cut the lemon skin in 1 cm (1/2-inch) wide slices and then cut each slice in two pieces. Return the livers to the pan. Add the whole olives and pickled lemon and leave to cook on high heat for 5–6 minutes. Stir two or three times during the cooking. The pan is left uncovered during the whole cooking. Spoon into a dish and serve hot. This can also be eaten cold.

olive rice Momo's way

Modern recipe:

SERVES 4 AS A SIDE DISH

250 g (9 oz) long-grain rice
1 green pepper
1 red pepper
100 g (3½ oz) stoned green olives
100 g (3½ oz) stoned black olives
100 ml (3½ fl oz) sunflower oil
1 onion, finely chopped
1 teaspoon salt
½ teaspoon ground white pepper
80 g (3 oz) unsalted butter

Preheat the oven to 180°C/350°F/Gas Mark 4. Put the rice in a measuring jug and check its volume. Remove the stalks and seeds from the peppers and cut them in small squares. Keep aside. Cut the green and black olives in thin slices and keep aside.

Heat the oil in a flameproof casserole dish and fry the onion gently until softened and translucent. Add the peppers and olives in the pan and fry for 2 minutes. Add the rice and stir it with the other ingredients until the rice grains are coated with the oil. Cover with water, using 1½ times the volume of the rice. Add the salt and pepper. Bring to the boil. Cover the pan and bake for 1 hour.

At the end of cooking, put the rice on a warm serving dish, cut the butter in small pieces and mix it in using a fork. Serve at once.

lamb boureks *with glazed carrots*

Modern recipe:

SERVES 4 AS A MAIN COURSE

For the glazed carrots:

3 large carrots

25 g (1 oz) unsalted butter

50 g (1³/₄ oz) brown sugar

¹/₄ teaspoon salt

For the filling:

100 g (3¹/₂ oz) unsalted butter

2 shallots, chopped

250 g (9 oz) boneless lamb, sliced finely

¹/₂ teaspoon salt

¹/₂ teaspoon ground white pepper

6 tablespoons finely chopped

flat-leaved parsley

100 g (3¹/₂ oz) blanched almonds

(see page 135), toasted and

coarsely crushed

For the boureks:

8 *ouarka* sheets (see page 70)

1 egg white, lightly beaten

oil, for deep-frying

Prepare the glazed carrots first. Peel and wash the carrots and slice them diagonally. Put them in a small pan, add water to cover and the butter, sugar and salt. Leave the carrots to cook uncovered on a low heat until the water has evaporated completely. Leave aside to cool.

Then prepare the *bourek* filling. Heat the butter in a pan and fry the shallots for 2 minutes. Then add the slices of lamb and let them cook for 4–5 minutes. Season with salt and pepper. Mix in the chopped parsley and almonds and put the stuffing aside to cool.

Cut each round *ouarka* sheet in half. Spread one semi-circle of *ouarka* on a working surface with the round edge towards you. Put one large tablespoon of the filling in a line on the sheet, close to the round edge. Fold the left and right sides of the sheet over the filling so that they exceed it by 5 mm (¹/₄ inch) on each side. Then roll the sheet round the filling. To seal the *bourek*, put a little egg white on the open edge of the *ouarka* to stick it on the roll. You should obtain cigars of 8 cm (3 inches) long and 2.5 cm (1 inch) diameter.

Heat the oil for deep-frying and deep-fry the *boureks* until golden brown and crisp, between 1 and 2 minutes. Drain on kitchen paper. Put four *boureks* on each serving and serve at once, with the preserved carrots on the side.

roasted sardines
with confit peppers

Modern recipes:

SERVES 4 AS A MAIN COURSE

4 large sardines, gutted, boned and
cleaned, with their heads

1 teaspoon salt

1/2 teaspoon ground white pepper

250 ml (9 fl oz) olive oil

2 red peppers

2 yellow peppers

3 garlic cloves, peeled

juice of 1 lemon

1 slice of rye bread, 1 cm (1/2 inch) thick

chermoula sauce (see page 80)

Preheat the oven to 130°C/250°F/Gas Mark 1/2.
Season the sardines inside and outside with three-
quarters of the salt and the pepper and keep aside
in a colander. Keep 3 tablespoons of olive oil to
season the peppers later.

Put the whole peppers and garlic cloves in an
ovenproof dish and pour the remaining olive oil
over them. Cover with foil and bake for an hour.
Leave until cool enough to handle, reserving the
roasting oil.

Turn up the oven to 200°C/400°F/Gas Mark 6.
Peel and de-seed the peppers and then cut the flesh
into strips. Season the peppers with the 3 tablespoons
of olive oil, the lemon juice and the remaining salt.
Keep them at room temperature while you make
the sardines.

Cut the crusts off the bread slices. Thinly spread
the soft roasted garlic on to the slices of bread, then
cut four 3 cm (1 1/2-inch) squares of bread and discard
the rest. Spread the sardines on a wooden board with
the skin under, and make a 3 cm (1 1/2-inch) incision
in each sardine, near the tail. Spread the sardines
with *chermoula* sauce. Pour 3 tablespoons of the
olive oil from roasting into a small pan and heat it for
2 minutes. Then quickly dip the slices of bread in it.
Put one piece of bread near the sardine's head. Tuck
the head back over the bread and insert it into the
incision near the tail. Repeat with the remaining
sardines, *chermoula* sauce and bread. Place the
sardines on a baking tray brushed with a little oil
and bake for 4 minutes.

Serve the sardines on a bed of roasted pepper
strips.

boureks of crispy vegetables Momo's way

Modern recipe:

SERVES 4

100 ml (3¹/₂ fl oz) olive oil

1 onion, finely chopped

6 tablespoons finely chopped fresh flat-leaved parsley

3 carrots, peeled and cut into thin strips (*julienne*)

2 unpeeled courgettes, cut into strips (*julienne*)

250 g (9 oz) mushroom caps, sliced

¹/₂ teaspoon salt

¹/₂ teaspoon ground white pepper

4 *ouarka* pastry sheets (see page 70)

1 tablespoon sherry vinegar

10 g (¹/₄ oz) sesame seeds

salt and pepper

Set aside 2 tablespoons of olive oil and heat the rest in a large frying-pan. Add the onion and cook until it starts to soften, without colouring. Set aside 2 teaspoons of chopped parsley and one quarter of the carrot and courgette *julienne* and add the rest of the courgettes and carrots, plus the mushrooms, to the frying-pan. Fry quickly while stirring and on high heat for 3–4 minutes to keep the vegetables crisp. One minute before finishing the cooking, add the parsley and half the salt and pepper. Remove the vegetables from the pan and leave to cool. Keep aside.

Preheat the oven to 180°C/350°F/Gas Mark 4.

Make three strips 5 cm (2 inches) wide from each pastry sheet and cut one end of each strip with a diagonal edge. Put a large spoonful of the vegetable filling at one end of one strip and then fold the pastry sheet over and over to make a triangular-shaped parcel. Repeat to make 12 *boureks*.

Put the *boureks* on a greased baking sheet and bake in the oven until crisp and golden on both sides, 10–15 minutes.

Meanwhile, combine the remaining uncooked carrot and courgette *julienne* in a bowl with the reserved oil and the sherry vinegar and season with salt and pepper to taste.

In a dry frying-pan, put the sesame seeds and, stirring with a wooden spoon, toast until golden.

Put the salad in the middle of the serving dishes, sprinkle over the reserved fresh chopped parsley and a pinch of sesame seeds and arrange three *boureks* around the salad. Serve hot.

lamb ribs
in a coriander crust

Modern recipe:

SERVES 4 AS A MAIN COURSE

For the breadcrumbs:

1/2 baguette or other white loaf

6 tablespoons finely chopped
fresh coriander

2 soup spoons olive oil

1/2 teaspoon salt

1/2 teaspoon ground white pepper

For the ribs:

100 ml (3 1/2 fl oz) sunflower oil

12 lamb ribs

1 teaspoon salt

1/2 teaspoon ground white pepper

2 soup spoons Dijon mustard

50 g (1 3/4 oz) butter

Twenty-four hours before you want to cook the dish, put the bread in a dry place for it to become very dry and crisp.

The next day, make the bread into crumbs, as fine as possible, in a food processor or blender. Add the coriander and oil, season with salt and pepper and mix thoroughly.

In a large pan, heat the sunflower oil. Remove the excess fat from the lamb ribs and trim the meat off the ends of the bones, as you would for a rack of lamb. Season the lamb ribs and add them to the frying-pan. Let them brown on all sides for about 5 minutes. Then remove them from the heat and let them rest, covered with foil, for 15 minutes.

Spread the ribs with mustard on both sides and coat them in the coriander crumbs. Then heat the butter in a frying-pan on a very low heat and cook the ribs for 1 minute on each side. Serve hot.

This dish is delicious served with Potato Gratin with Fresh Coriander (see page 100) or Fennel and Courgette Compote with Aniseed (see page 98). You can also serve it with couscous (see page 115).

rose-petal water tabbouleh
with fresh fruit

Modern recipe:

SERVES 4

250 g (9 oz) couscous

150 ml (1/4 pint) rose-petal water

2 kiwi fruits

1/4 medium-size fresh pineapple

100 g (3 1/2 oz) strawberries, hulled

2 soup spoons icing sugar

juice of 2 limes

Prepare and cook the couscous as explained on page 115. Add half the rose-petal water, mix and leave until cool.

Peel and dice the kiwi fruits. Peel the pineapple, remove the woody central core and dice the flesh. Cut the strawberries in slices.

Mix the kiwi fruit, pineapple and strawberries in a bowl. Sprinkle with the icing sugar, add the remaining rose-petal water and pour on the lime juice. Mix well and leave to macerate in the fridge for 30 minutes.

Gently mix two-thirds of the fruit with the couscous and put the mixture on a serving dish in a mound with a well in the middle. Put the remaining fruit in the centre and serve at once.

couscous with partridges

Traditional recipe:

SERVES 6 AS A MAIN COURSE

200 g (7^1/$_2$ oz) dried beans
3 partridges
1 teaspoon salt
^{1}/$_2$ teaspoon ground white pepper
100 ml (3^1/$_2$ fl oz) tablespoons
sunflower oil
3 onions, finely chopped
4 garlic cloves, finely chopped
1 teaspoon paprika
^{1}/$_4$ teaspoon Cayenne pepper (optional)
^{1}/$_2$ teaspoon coarse salt
2.5 litres (4^1/$_2$ pints) water
2 green peppers, de-seeded
and quartered
1 kg (2^1/$_4$ lb) couscous
75 g (2^3/$_4$ oz) unsalted butter
salt and pepper

The day before, put the dried beans into cold water and leave to soak overnight. The next day, sprinkle the partridges inside and outside with salt and pepper. Heat the oil in a large pan or the base of a *couscoussier* and fry the partridges on low heat and on all sides until golden. Remove the partridges, keep them aside and add the onion and garlic to the pan. Fry until soft and golden. Add the drained beans, all the spices and the coarse salt, pour in the water and bring to the boil, covered. Fit the upper part (or a steamer) on top, in order to steam the couscous as explained on page 115.

After 30 minutes, add the partridges and the peppers to the stock and leave to cook for 1 more hour, while steaming the couscous above the stock.

Remove the partridges from the stock with a slotted spoon and leave the stock on high heat for 10 minutes to allow it to reduce a little. Taste the stock and correct the seasoning to taste.

Put the partridges in the centre of a large serving plate, surround them with the couscous, soak with one or two ladles of stock and top the couscous with the beans and peppers. Serve the remaining stock in a bowl.

COUSCOUS with steamed green vegetables and buttermilk

This is a Berber recipe.

Traditional recipe:

SERVES 6 AS A MAIN COURSE

For the green vegetables:

4 unpeeled courgettes, halved lengthways and cut into 5 cm (2-inch) pieces

400 g (14 oz) shelled green peas

400 g (14 oz) shelled broad beans

1 teaspoon salt

$1/2$ teaspoon ground white pepper

75 g ($2^3/4$ oz) butter

For the couscous:

1 kg ($2^1/4$ lb) medium-grain couscous

800 ml (1 pint 7 fl oz) water

1 teaspoon salt

80 g (3 oz) unsalted butter, cut into pieces

buttermilk, to serve

Steam the courgettes for 10 minutes and keep aside. Steam the peas and broad beans for 10 minutes, then remove and discard the broad bean skin by pinching between your fingers.

Steam the couscous as explained on page 115. In a bowl, mix the three vegetables, season with salt and pepper and add the butter pieces and steam for 2 more minutes.

Put the couscous on a warm serving dish and the green vegetables on another warm serving dish. Serve at once, accompanied with buttermilk. The buttermilk can be either used as a drink or to pour on the dish.

couscous of barley

Traditional recipe:

SERVES 6 AS A MAIN COURSE

100 g (3½ oz) dried broad beans

100 g (3½ oz) chick-peas

500 g (1 lb 2 oz) lean beef

1 teaspoon salt

½ teaspoon ground white pepper

100 ml (3½ fl oz) olive oil

2 green peppers

2 aubergines

2 courgettes

2 large tomatoes

3 carrots

3 turnips

1 onion

500 g (1 lb 2 oz) swiss chard

1 teaspoon paprika

¼ teaspoon Cayenne pepper

½ teaspoon ground turmeric

1 tablespoon concentrated
tomato purée

1 kg (2¼ lb) barley grits (crushed barley)

50 g (1¾ oz) butter

The day before, put the dried broad beans and the chick-peas separately into cold water and leave to soak overnight.

The next day, cut the meat into medium-size cubes and sprinkle with salt and pepper. Heat the oil in a large pan and fry the chunks of meat on all sides on low heat until golden.

In the meantime, prepare all the vegetables: cut the peppers in quarters, removing the stalks and seeds; peel the aubergines and cut into large chunks; leave courgettes unpeeled and halve them lengthways and then into large chunks; leave tomatoes unpeeled and quarter them; peel carrots and cut into large sticks; peel and quarter turnips; chop the onion and cut the white parts of the swiss chard into large chunks (the green parts can be used in another recipe).

Once it's completely browned, remove the meat and set aside and add the onion to the pan. Fry until soft and golden. Add the drained broad beans and chick-peas, all the spices and the tomato purée diluted in a little water, cover with water and bring to the boil. Cover and cook for half an hour.

After 30 minutes, add the meat chunks and the vegetables, except the tomatoes, courgettes and aubergines, and leave to cook for 30 more minutes. If necessary, add more water to cover the vegetables

After 30 minutes, add the tomatoes, courgettes and aubergines and leave to cook for 30 more minutes.

Steam the barley grits three times, over the stock, as if it were couscous, as explained on page 115. After the last steaming, add the butter and mix it into the barley.

Taste the stock and correct the seasoning to taste.

Put the barley in a dome shape in a large serving plate. Soak with a couple of ladles of stock, add the meat in the centre and surround with the vegetables. Serve the remaining stock in a tureen.

Olive press, Kabylie

vermicelli dessert
with almonds and cinnamon

Traditional recipe:

SERVES 4

250 g (9 oz) very thin vermicelli
$1/4$ teaspoon salt
1 tablespoon sunflower oil
60 g (2 oz) butter
50 g ($1^3/4$ oz) blanched almonds
(see page 135)
100 ml ($3^1/2$ fl oz) orange-blossom water
80 g (3 oz) icing sugar
1 tablespoon ground cinnamon
1 litre ($1^3/4$ pints) buttermilk
(optional), to serve

Toast the vermicelli lightly on very low heat, in a dry frying-pan. Remove from the pan and leave to cool. Crush the vermicelli very coarsely with your hand. Add a pinch of salt and the oil. Mix together.

Heat a teaspoon of butter in a frying-pan and fry the almonds until golden. Leave to cool and then chop the almonds coarsely.

Boil water in a steamer and steam the vermicelli for 3 minutes. Put the vermicelli on a plate, add 3 tablespoonfuls of cold water and leave to swell for 5 minutes. Repeat the two previous operations twice. Cut the remaining butter in small pieces and add it to the vermicelli. Keep aside 1 tablespoon of icing sugar and a third of the ground cinnamon. Then add the almonds, the orange-blossom water, the remaining icing sugar and the remaining ground cinnamon to the vermicelli and mix together.

Serve warm on a plate in a dome shape and decorate in the pattern of your choice with the remaining icing sugar and ground cinnamon. Serve with the buttermilk, if using, in a carafe.

red peppers preserved in olive oil

Traditional recipe:
20 large red peppers
1 teaspoon salt
olive oil, to cover

Preheat the oven to 180°C/350°F/Gas Mark 4. Roast the peppers on all sides, in the preheated oven, for 20 minutes, until the skin gets black. Remove from the oven, wrap them in a plastic bag so that they are easier to peel and leave to cool.

Once cool, peel them thoroughly and remove the seeds and stalks. Sprinkle a little salt on each pepper, put them in a large strainer and leave to drain for 3 hours.

Prepare a large clean wooden board. Cut each pepper in four strips, lengthways, dry with kitchen paper and spread all the peppers on the board. Put the board in the sun, slightly slanted to allow any excess pepper juice to run away and leave to dry in the sun for 3 hours. Turn the peppers upside-down on the board and leave to dry in the sun for 3 more hours.

Put the peppers in a clean 500 ml (18 fl oz) jar with an airtight lid and cover with olive oil.

This recipe is excellent but can only be made on a bright sunny day as, once grilled, the peppers must dry in the sun. Preserved red peppers can be kept, fully covered with olive oil, for several months. They are eaten as a starter, sprinkled with a little salt and chopped garlic, or as part of a cold mixed grilled vegetables starter with aubergines, courgettes and sun-dried tomatoes, or in a fresh tomato salad. Also delicious hot if you fry them quickly and add two or three fried eggs.

It is far easier for a sieve to hold water than for a woman to trust a man.

Arabic proverb

WINES AND DRINKS

Wines are proscribed in Muslim law. However, North Africa, particularly Algeria
and Morocco, are great wine producers. Their wines include the Guerouane,
the Sidi Brahim, the Mascara and the Boulaouane, and are widely exported.

Since they are forbidden wine, North Africans have taken advantage of the abundance of delicious fruits to
create a whole range of original and refreshing soft beverages using fruit, milk, fragrant waters and spices.
Despite an invasion of western sodas, it is still possible to find natural drinks in any cafe or home.
These drinks include: fresh juices made from oranges, grapes, watermelons, pomegranates, lemons;
almond milks with cinnamon; and chilled rose-water drinks.

Momo's cocktails

Marrakech O'Marrakech

Shake up some fresh mint with some ice. Add 20 ml white rum, the juice of $^1/4$ lime, 10 ml lemon juice
and 10 ml sugar syrup. Shake and strain into a champagne flute. Top up with champagne.

Momo's Special

Shake up some fresh mint with some ice. Add 50 ml vodka, 15 ml sugar syrup and 15 ml lemon juice.
Shake and pour into a glass. Top up with soda.

The Touareg

Shake up some ice with the juice of $^1/2$ lime. Add 50 ml Morgan's Spiced Rum,
3 dashes of angostura bitters, a dash of lime cordial and 15 ml lemon juice.
Shake and pour into a glass. Top up with ginger beer.

From left to right: Marrakech O'Marrakech; Momo's Special; The Touareg

SET MENUS

Easy to make menu I
starter: Merk *Hzina* Salad (page 65)
main course: Whiting Balls in Tomato and Pepper Sauce (page 88)
dessert: Orange Salad with Cinnamon (page 122)

Easy to make menu II
starter: Carrot Salad with Orange Juice and
Orange-Blossom Water (page 61)
main course: Kefta with Eggs (page 200)
dessert: Dried Fruit Salad with Aromatic Spices (page 173)

Spring menu
starter: Boureks of Crispy Vegetables (page 207)
main course: Lhem Lahlou (page 199)
dessert: Milk *Pastilla* (page 128)

Summer menu
starter: Pigeon *Pastilla* (page 77)
main course: King Prawn *Tagine* with Braised Fennel (page 82)
dessert: Couscous *Seffa* (page 127)

Autumn menu
starter: Roasted Prawns with Cumin served on a Carrot
and Orange Salad (page 165)
main course: Confit of Duck *Tagine* with Pears, Figs
and Glazed Carrots (page 112)
dessert: Orange Salad with Cinnamon (page 122)

Winter menu
starter: Harira (page 68)
main course: Fillet of John Dory with Confit Aubergines
and Polenta (page 91)
dessert: Dried Fruit Salad with Aromatic Spices (page 173)

Moroccan menu
starter: Briouats of Saffron Chicken (page 73)
with *Mechouia* (page 62)
main course: Monkfish *Tagine* with Pickled Lemon (page 80)
dessert: Tart with *Mroziya* (page 130)

Algerian menu
starter: Chorba Frik (page 195)
main course: Kefta with Eggs (page 200)
dessert: Vermicelli Dessert with Almonds and Cinnamon (page 214)

Tunisian Menu
starter: Tuna and Egg *Brik* (page 156)
main course: Tagine Mqualli of Beef and Fennel (page 160)
dessert: Makroude with Dates (page 182)

Modern recipe menu I
starter: Roasted Prawns with Cumin served on a
Carrot and Orange Salad (page 165)
main course: Lamb ribs in a Coriander Crust (page 208)
with Potato Gratin (page 100)
dessert: Pastilla of Fresh Pineapple with a
Red Fruit *Coulis* (page 125)

Modern recipe menu II
starter: Lamb *Boureks* with Glazed Carrots (page 203)
main course: Sea Bass Fillet served on a Warm *Tabbouleh*
with Citrus Fruit Juice (page 166)
dessert: Croustillants of Roasted Figs with Almonds
and Cinnamon (page 176)

Family menu
starter: Couscous Salad in *Tabbouleh* Style (page 192)
main course: Sea Bass *Tagine* with Potatoes (page 84)
dessert: Jabane (page 133)

Buffet menu for a dinner party
starters: Kemia including *Mhemmer* (page 64), *Zaalouk* (page 63), Four Flavour Salad (page 58), Tomato *Confit* with
Golden Sesame Seeds (page 56), Fresh Broad Bean Salad (page 154), Assortment of Olives (page 154)
main courses: Couscous with Seven Vegetables (page 171) served with *Brochettes* of Lamb and Chicken (page 117)
desserts: an assortment of pastries including Gazelle Horns (page 131), *Feqquas* (page 132), *Briouats* of Almond Paste (page 134),
Montecaos (page 178), Candied Grapefruit Peel (page 139)
Served with Mint Tea (page 144) and chilled Almond Milk (page 143)

A GLOSSARY OF MAGHREBI COOKING EQUIPMENT

Couscoussier The *couscoussier* is used to cook the whole couscous dish. The meat and vegetables are cooked in the stock in the lower part of the *couscoussier*, while the couscous grains are steamed in the upper part. The lower part is called a *quedra* or *tenjra* and the upper part is called a *keskas*. A conventional steamer can replace the couscoussier, provided the holes are small enough – you don't want the couscous grains falling into the stock. The upper part used to be a woven straw bowl and the lower part was an earthenware stockpot.

Gharbal Sieve.

Gsaa A large deep dish. Used to prepare couscous or bread dough. Usually made of wood, earthenware or metal.

Kanoun Round earthenware brazier or grill. Used with charcoal to cook *tagines* or boil water to make mint tea. Exists in all sizes.

Khabia Large earthenware jars, glazed on the inside and used to keep *confit* meat, olives, olive oil or pickled vegetables.

Kissan dila atai Mint tea glasses. Either small or large. Mint tea is traditionally served in a slightly slanted glass either in plain glass or in bright green, red or blue glass, richly decorated with patterns of gold. Mint tea is never served in a cup. The glass is not filled completely and tea is poured from high up so that large bubbles form on the surface.

M'ghazel Kebab skewers. Usually long and made of metal. They are used to make *brochettes*. Wooden skewers are just as good, particularly if you are not cooking over charcoal.

Mehraz Pestle and mortar. Usually made of heavy brass.

Mida Table. In North Africa people typically eat at low tables.

Mijmar Rectangular brazier or grill. Used with charcoal to grill the *brochettes* and *keftas*. Sardines are cooked on a special metal grill called a *chouaya*.

Mqla Frying pan. From *mqla* comes the word *mqualli* which is given to those dishes with a reduced and thickened sauce.

Siniya A large round or oval metal tray (usually copper or silver), traditionally used to serve mint tea and pastries. The *siniya* is also the tray containing all the symbols of the Jewish Passover tradition, in memory of the long slavery of the Jews in Egypt. It is part the *Sedder* table. Each symbol (hard-boiled egg, *harosset*, romaine lettuce, lamb shoulder bone and flesh, *matzoth* and celery sticks or bitter herbs with very salted water) is put in a small dish.

Tagine Usually called *tagine slaoui*. Round earthenware glazed dish with a cone-shaped lid. Exists in all sizes. Used both to cook and to serve all the meat, fish and poultry *tagine* dishes.

Tbeck Large round woven straw plate. Used to sort couscous grains or pulses.

Tbicka Round woven deep straw basket with a cone-shaped lid, used to prevent bread from drying.

BOOKS

Cookbooks and the food of North Africa

Ahmed Laasri, *240 recettes de Cuisine Marocaine* (Editions Jacques Grancher)

Maguy Kakon, *La Cuisine Juive du Maroc de Mère en Fille* (Editions Daniel Briand)

Fatima-Zohra Bouayed, *La Cuisine Algerienne* (Editions ENAG)

Mme Z. Sekelli, *L'Art Culinaire à travers l'Algérie* (SNED, Alger)

Edmond Zeitoun, *250 Recettes de Cuisine Tunisienne*, 1982 (Editions Jacques Grancher)

Mohamed Kouki, *650 Recettes Cuisine et Pâtisserie Tunisiennes* (Ommok Sannafa)

Kitty Morse, *The Vegetarian Table – North Africa*, 1996 (Chronicle Books San Francisco)

Maguelonne Toussaint-Samat, *Couscous*, 1994 (Editions Casterman Avril)

Sarah Woodward, *Moorish Food*, 1998 (Kyle Cathie Limited)

Magali Morsy, *Recettes de Couscous*, 1996 (Edisud)

Fiction, history and proverbs

Isabelle Eberhardt, *Au Pays des Sables*

Alexandre Dumas, *Adventures in Algeria*

Albert Camus, *La Peste*, 1947; *L'Etranger*, 1942

Paul Bowles, *The Sheltering Sky*, 1949

Martin Stone, *The Agony of Algeria*, 1997

Henry Munson Jr, *The House of Si Abd Allah – The Oral History of a Moroccan Family*

Arthur Leared, *Morocco and the Moors*, 1985

Louis Brunot, *Au seuil de la vie marocaine*

Leila Messaoudi, *Proverbes et dictons du Maroc* (Editions Belvisi)

Anis Freyha, *A Dictionary of Modern Lebanese Proverbs*, 1983 (Librairie du Liban Beirut)

Patrick Dubreucq, *Alexandre Roubtzoff: Une vie en Tunisie* (ACR Edition)

Koudir Benchikou and Denise Brahim, *Etienne Dinet* (ACR Edition)

GENERAL INDEX

RECIPE INDEX

Acknowledgements

Mourad Mazouz wishes to thank M Ahmed Benyamina, the Algerian Ambassador in London; Mr Ali El Kasmi, the Director of the Moroccan National Tourist Office in London; Mr Houssem Ben Azouz, the Director of the Tunisian National Tourist Office in London; Hakim Mazouz; his son, Lounès; Jonathan Amar; Ahmed Benbadryef; Marie Valensi; his father and brothers in Algeria; Laura Tolède; Jo Bowlby; Anouschka Menzies; Hénya Mekki; Stuart Goldman; Djaouad Kadiri; and a very special thanks to Tunisair.

The publishers wish to thank Jane Humphrey, Anouschka Menzies and all at Bacchus, Laurent Guinci, Aruna Mathur, Mark Foster, Neil Saville, and all at Momo.

Photography credits: Mark Luscombe-Whyte: cover and backcover photographs; endpaper images; photographs on pages 2-3, 4, 9, 11, 13, 15, 18-19, 23, 27, 28, 30-1, 38, 40, 45, 47, 48, 49, 53, 60 (top left; bottom left; bottom right), 67, 79, 81 (top left; top right; bottom right), 86-7, 99 (top left; top right; bottom right), 102-3, 124, 129 (top left; bottom right), 140, 147, 149, 158 (top left; top right; bottom right), 161, 167 (top left; top right), 179, 180 (top left; top right), 183, 185, 186, 188-9, 213.
Jean Cazals: photographs on pages 57, 60 (top right), 72, 75, 76, 81 (bottom left), 83, 90, 94, 99 (bottom left), 104, 109, 113, 118, 123, 126, 129 (top right; bottom left), 136, 145, 152, 157, 158 (bottom right), 167 (bottom left; bottom right), 169, 170, 172, 174, 177, 180 (bottom right), 193, 194, 198, 205, 206, 217.
Marie Valensi: photograph on page 180 (bottom left)